RENAISSANCE

VOLUME 6

Language — Merchants

GROLIER
EDUCATIONAL

Published by Grolier Educational
Sherman Turnpike
Danbury, Connecticut 06816

© 2002 Brown Partworks Limited

Set ISBN 0-7172-5673-1
Volume 6 ISBN 0-7172-5668-5

Library of Congress Cataloging-in-Publication Data

Renaissance.
    p. cm.
Summary: Chronicles the cultural and artistic flowering
known as the Renaissance that flourished in Europe and
in other parts of the world from approximately 1375 to
1575 A.D.
Includes index.
Contents: v. 1. Africa–Bologna — v. 2. Books and libraries–
Constantinople — v. 3. Copernicus–Exploration — v. 4.
Eyck–Government — v. 5. Guilds and crafts–Landscape
painting — v. 6. Language–Merchants — v. 7. Michelangelo–
Palaces and villas — v. 8. Palestrina–Reformation — v. 9.
Religious dissent–Tapestry — v. 10. Technology–Zwingli.
    ISBN 0-7172-5673-1 (set : alk. paper)
    1. Renaissance—Juvenile literature. [1. Renaissance.]
I. Grolier Educational (Firm)
    CB361 .R367 2002
    940.2'1—dc21
                                    2002002477

For information address the publisher:
Grolier Educational, Sherman Turnpike,
Danbury, Connecticut 06816

FOR BROWN PARTWORKS

Project Editor: Shona Grimbly
Deputy Editor: Rachel Bean
Text Editor: Chris King
Designer: Sarah Williams
Picture Research: Veneta Bullen
Maps: Colin Woodman
Design Manager: Lynne Ross
Production: Matt Weyland
Managing Editor: Tim Cooke
Consultant: Stephen A. McKnight
                         University of Florida

Printed and bound in Singapore

ABOUT THIS BOOK

This is one of a set of 10 books that tells the story of the Renaissance—a time of discovery and change in the world. It was during this period—roughly from 1375 to 1575—that adventurous mariners from Europe sailed the vast oceans in tiny ships and found the Americas and new sea routes to the Spice Islands of the East. The influx of gold and silver from the New World and the increase in trade made many merchants and traders in Europe extremely rich. They spent some of their wealth on luxury goods like paintings and gold and silver items for their homes, and this created a new demand for the work of artists of all kinds. Europe experienced a cultural flowering as great artists like Leonardo da Vinci, Michelangelo, and Raphael produced masterpieces that have never been surpassed.

At the same time, scholars were rediscovering the works of the ancient Greek and Roman writers, and this led to a new way of looking at the world based on observation and the importance of the individual. This humanism, together with other new ideas, spread more rapidly than ever before thanks to the development of printing with movable type.

There was upheaval in the church too. Thinkers such as Erasmus and Luther began to question the teachings of the established church, and this eventually led to a breakaway from the Catholic church and the setting up of Protestant churches—an event called the Reformation.

The set focuses on Europe, but it also looks at how societies in other parts of the world such as Africa, China, India, and the Americas were developing, and the ways in which the Islamic and Christian worlds interacted.

The entries in this set are arranged alphabetically and are illustrated with paintings, photographs, drawings, and maps, many from the Renaissance period. Each entry ends with a list of cross-references to other entries in the set, and at the end of each book there is a timeline to help you relate events to one another in time.

There is also a useful "Further Reading" list that includes websites, a glossary of special terms, and an index covering the whole set.

Contents

VOLUME 6

Language

During the Middle Ages most scholars and priests wrote and even spoke in Latin—the language that was originally used by the ancient Romans. Vernacular, or ordinary, languages such as French or Italian were considered inferior for anything except everyday use.

Latin was the language of the Christian church, used for religious rites and in the standard translation of the Bible. Because so many scholars were also clergymen, Latin was also the language of philosophy, science, and other kinds of learning. In addition it was the language of politics and law.

USING THE VERNACULAR

Toward the end of the Middle Ages poets and writers increasingly chose to write in their own language. This allowed them to help shape a distinct national literary culture and also to reach a wider, less scholarly audience. The Italian poets Dante (1265–1321) and Petrarch (1304–1374) were among the first writers to use Italian as a written language. For Dante the use of the vernacular language heralded a new age in which ordinary people would be literate (able to read).

In some ways the ideas of humanist scholars seemed to go against those of Dante. While they disliked medieval culture, the humanists delighted in writing and speaking Latin. Indeed, Latin continued to be used throughout the Renaissance, partly because it enabled scholars across Europe to communicate in a common language.

Despite the humanist revival of classical (ancient Greek and Roman) learning, the vernacular languages came to be more widely used in the Renaissance. As literacy spread and the invention of the printing press brought books to an ever wider audience, authors wrote in their own languages to reach more people. For many writers using their own language was tied up with pride in their country's culture. Gradually, writing in vernacular languages also helped to standardize those languages, which before had often varied greatly within a country.

The religious reformers of the Renaissance also argued for the use of vernacular languages because they believed that ordinary people should be able to read the Bible for themselves. Many vernacular translations of the Bible were made during this time.

Above: A page from a 15th-century manuscript edition of Il Canzoniere, *a set of poems by Petrarch, who was one of the first poets to write in Italian.*

SEE ALSO

♦ Books and Libraries
♦ Dante
♦ Erasmus
♦ Humanism
♦ Literacy
♦ Literature
♦ Petrarch
♦ Poetry
♦ Printing

Leo X

ope Leo X (1475–1521) is perhaps best remembered for the lavish nature of his lifestyle and for the fact that his papacy coincided with the birth of the Protestant Reformation. A generous patron of the arts, Leo was responsible for commissioning Raphael to work on the church of Saint Peter's in Rome. However, Leo lived at a time when there was considerable resentment at the wealth and extravagance of church officials. This resentment fueled the spread of Protestantism.

Leo X's real name was Giovanni de Medici. He was the second son of Lorenzo the Magnificent, who was the rich, powerful ruler of Florence. The young Giovanni received the best education Europe could offer and was taught privately by learned tutors. Giovanni entered the church and by the time he was 17 years old had been made a cardinal. For the next 20 years he traveled widely in Europe, becoming more experienced in church affairs and developing his interests in art and literature. He was also involved in his family's struggle to remain the dominant force in Florence.

ELECTION AS POPE

When Pope Julius II died in 1513, Giovanni was elected Pope Leo X at the age of 38. His coronation was a marvelous spectacle and hinted at the lavish lifestyle he was to lead in office. Dressed in snowy white robes and mounted on a white horse, the new pope rode through the streets of Rome

accompanied by about 250 cardinals, bishops, and other churchmen, as well as soldiers, flag-bearers, and servants. The procession was cheered by huge crowds, and the streets were adorned with works of art, such as paintings, sculptures, and newly built arches.

Leo had a great interest in the arts and made Rome the center of Italian culture. He encouraged scholars, teachers, and writers to come to Rome. Many of them relied entirely on the pope's money. He also supported the leading painters and sculptors of the

Above: This portrait of Leo X is by Raphael, one of many artists to enjoy the pope's patronage. Leo is pictured with two of his cardinals.

day, including the artist Raphael, whom he commissioned to produce cartoons, or initial drawings, for tapestries to decorate the Sistine Chapel in the Vatican. When the architect Bramante died in 1514, Leo put Raphael in charge of building the new basilica (church) of Saint Peter's.

Leo's extravagance with money was not just restricted to his patronage of the arts. He indulged himself with

---

Leo's extravagance with money was not restricted to his patronage of the arts

---

Below: This painting by Giorgio Vasari shows Leo parading through the streets of Florence. Leo was famous for his extravagant displays of wealth.

many forms of costly entertainments and amusements, such as bullfighting, theatrical and musical performances, and carnivals. He also loved to go hunting, and in one year hunted solidly

for more than a month. He held large banquets at which guests ate rare delicacies and were entertained by musicians, clowns, and jesters. Because of such extravagance the papacy built up large debts during Leo's reign.

A SKILLED POLITICIAN

In politics Leo proved to be a cunning operator who was skillful at negotiating. His main aim was to preserve the papacy's power in Italy against the threat posed by foreign powers such as France and Spain, and by Italian city-states like Venice. Leo's policy was to shift his support from one side to another to prevent any single power from becoming too strong. In this he was generally successful.

In 1516, when the French had become the dominant force in northern Italy, he signed an important agreement—known as the French Concordat—with Francis I, the king of France. This agreement gave French

monarchs much greater influence over the regulation of church affairs in France. For example, it allowed them to choose who became bishops or abbots, rather than leaving the decision to the pope—though the pope still had to approve their choices. In 1519 Leo signed a treaty with Francis to combat the power of the Holy Roman emperor Charles V. However, two years later he changed policy and formed an alliance with the emperor to rid Italy of the French.

CHURCH CORRUPTION

While Leo was preoccupied with the political and military dangers posed by France and Spain, another threat to the papacy was developing in northern Europe. Here many people resented both the wealth of senior church officials and the extent to which they were involved in everyday politics.

This general feeling of resentment found a focus in the issue of the sale of indulgences, documents that, according to Catholic doctrine, freed the owner from suffering in purgatory for his or her sins. In 1515 Leo authorized Archbishop Albrecht of Mainz to sell indulgences. The money raised was used partly to pay for the building of Saint Peter's in Rome and partly to pay off Albrecht's huge debts.

One man who was particularly angered by this action was the German monk Martin Luther (1483–1546). Luther believed that there was nothing in the Bible that justified the sale of indulgences. In protest he wrote 95 theses (articles) arguing in favor of church reform and nailed them to the door of the church in Wittenburg.

Distracted by the political situation in Italy and his cultural pursuits, Leo did not take Luther's threat seriously. Faced with his challenge, Leo simply ordered the head of Luther's order, the Augustinians, to discipline the monk. This measure proved to be ineffective, and Luther's views became extremely popular, spreading quickly across northern Europe.

Eventually, in 1520, Leo was forced to issue a papal bull (or document) condemning Luther for heresy. When Luther refused to bow to the authority of the pope, Leo excommunicated him—that is, expelled him from the church by preventing him from taking part in its sacraments or rites. However, the pope had acted too late. By the time Leo died of malaria in 1521, the Protestant Reformation had already taken root.

Above: Francis I of France kneels before Leo in 1516. The two leaders later made an important alliance.

Leonardo da Vinci

Above: This chalk drawing is thought to be a self-portrait made by Leonardo in about 1513, when he was in his sixties. It shows him as an elderly man with flowing hair and beard.

architect, a scientist, an engineer, and a thinker. He designed countless new inventions and made thousands of studies of the natural world, including the most advanced drawings of human anatomy of the time.

Leonardo's boundless curiosity often left him with little time to paint. Today only about 25 paintings by him survive, about a third of which are unfinished. Few of his engineering projects were actually carried out, and he published none of his writings. Nevertheless, Leonardo's versatility makes him the outstanding example of the humanists' ideal of the "universal man"—someone who excelled in the arts and sciences.

THE YOUNG FLORENTINE

Leonardo was born on April 15, 1452, in a small country town named Vinci near Florence. His father, Ser Piero da Vinci, was the town notary, or legal officer, and his mother, Caterina, was a local peasant. Although Leonardo was illegitimate, he was brought up by Ser Piero and his younger, well-born wife.

When Leonardo was 16 or so, his father moved to Florence—at that time a bustling center not only of trade and industry but also of the arts. The city was ruled by a powerful banking family, the Medici, who used their wealth to build new palaces, squares, and streets as well as to commission, or order, works from the leading painters and sculptors of the day.

Leonardo had already shown an extraordinary talent for drawing, and his father entered him as an apprentice in the workshop of one of Florence's

Leonardo da Vinci (1452–1518) is one of the world's most famous artists, and his painting the *Mona Lisa* is one of the best-known works of art. Leonardo was a celebrity in his lifetime, and just a few years after his death the painter and art historian Giorgio Vasari (1511–1574) hailed him as a genius. Leonardo was not only a painter but a musician, an

NOTEBOOKS AND SKETCHBOOKS

During his lifetime Leonardo made many drawings and filled hundreds of sketchbooks. He also kept a succession of notebooks, which together total more than 6,000 pages. Many of these works survive and provide insights into Leonardo's endlessly inquisitive mind. They are crammed with drawings and his tiny handwriting. At first the writing seems illegible, but in fact it is simply back to front, as if seen in a mirror. It seems likely that Leonardo wrote in this way not to keep his ideas secret—the writing is easily read with a mirror—but because he was left-handed and did not want to make smudges as his hand passed over the wet ink.

Together Leonardo's sketches and notes show an extraordinary mixture of imagination and observation. They include designs for weapons and other fantastic inventions, and also meticulous drawings of plants, animals, fossils, the human body, and other aspects of the natural world. Sometimes he placed the fantastic and the realistic side by side—one page included a picture of a dragon among studies of cats fighting.

Right: A page of Leonardo's plant studies. The main drawing shows a plant called the Star of Bethlehem.

leading artists, the sculptor and painter Andrea del Verrocchio (about 1435–1488). Apprentices often helped their master carry out commissions, and according to Vasari Leonardo was responsible for painting a kneeling angel in one of Verrocchio's altarpieces. The story goes that Verrocchio was so impressed by his pupil's work and so ashamed of his own by comparison that he promptly decided to give up painting altogether.

In 1472 Leonardo was accepted as a member of the Florentine painters' guild. Although that gave him the right to work as an independent painter, he remained in Verrocchio's workshop, helping him with his commissions. He also produced his own smaller works, like the *Madonna Benois* (about 1478),

a painting of the Virgin Mary and the baby Jesus. Earlier Italian painters had often depicted Mary as an imposing queen. Leonardo, by contrast, showed her almost as if she were an ordinary young mother, laughing and playing with her child. In this respect he was influenced by the paintings of northern European artists, and he was also influenced by their use of oil paint. Leonardo was among the first Italian artists to adopt oil paint, which he used to create rich, dark colors and to achieve a subtle blending of tones that became a hallmark of his style.

By the late 1470s Leonardo was running his own workshop, and in 1481 he received his first important commission. It was for a painting to decorate an altar and shows the

MASTERPIECE: *THE LAST SUPPER*

Leonardo's *The Last Supper* is a huge painting that stretches across the wall of the refectory, or dining hall, of the Santa Maria delle Grazie monastery in Milan. Leonardo chose to portray the story of Christ's final meal before his trial and crucifixion at its most dramatic moment, when Christ foretells that one of the assembled disciples is about to betray him. He shows Christ sitting at the center of a long white-clothed table on which are the scattered remains of a meal. On either side of him are the disciples, each of whom expresses his shock at Christ's revelation in a strikingly different way. One reels back in horror, while others stare at each other in angry disbelief; another casts his eyes sadly down, while the traitor, Judas, starts back in terror.

Unusually, Leonardo did not show Christ and the assembled saints with golden haloes (circles of heavenly light) around their heads, which was the traditional way of showing holiness. Instead, he depicted them as ordinary human beings stirred by deep emotions. Similarly, the room shown in the painting seems to be a continuation of the refectory itself, so that the dining monks would have been encouraged to see the disciples as ordinary men like themselves, living—and eating—in the same world.

Below: Leonardo's **The Last Supper** *(1495–1497). The painting is in poor condition because Leonardo tried out new techniques that later proved unstable.*

adoration of the Magi, or the three kings visiting the newly born Jesus in the stable. Leonardo worked on the altarpiece for several months, but in 1482 abandoned it and left for Milan.

No one knows why Leonardo went to live and work in Milan. This city-state in the far north of Italy was ruled by Duke Ludovico Sforza (1452–1508), whose magnificent court rivaled that of the Medici in Florence. The duke was often at war, and in a letter to Ludovico Leonardo offered his services, primarily as a military engineer.

Leonardo in fact carried out little engineering work for the duke, although he filled his notebooks with ideas for weapons and fortifications. Ludovico was much more interested in Leonardo's skill as a painter. One of

Leonardo's first works for his new patron was a portrait of the duke's mistress, Cecilia Gallerani, whom he showed gently stroking a sleek white ermine, which was the Sforza emblem.

Leonardo also worked on plans for a bronze equestrian monument to commemorate Ludovico's father, Francesco (1401–1466)—equestrian monuments are sculptures of a soldier or ruler riding on horseback. Leonardo initially

---

The lifelike gestures and expressions in The Last Supper *brought Leonardo acclaim throughout Italy*

---

aimed to show Francesco's horse rearing on its hind legs. Given the weight of the sculpture, such a pose would have been a great technical achievement, never before realized in bronze. Leonardo's ambitious plans came to nothing, however, when the duke gave all his available bronze to his brother-in-law to make cannons for war. Leonardo's most important artwork for the Sforza was *The Last Supper* (1495–1497). The lifelike gestures and expressions depicted in the painting brought him acclaim throughout Italy.

THE WANDERING YEARS
In 1499 the French king Louis XII (reigned 1498–1515) occupied Milan, forcing Ludovico Sforza to flee. In search of a new patron Leonardo returned to his native city, Florence. For a while Leonardo served as an engineer in the service of the military commander Cesare Borgia (about 1475–1507). His job was to inspect fortifications throughout Tuscany and

Umbria, and to make military maps. Leonardo found little time for painting during this period. He did, however, begin and very nearly complete the celebrated portrait of a lady known as the *Mona Lisa* (1503–1506).

Leonardo, who was now more than 50 years old, also found he had a younger rival working in Florence: Michelangelo (1475–1564). The two painters disliked each other, and the Florentine government exploited their rivalry by inviting each of the artists to paint a wall of the city council chamber. Leonardo's subject was a famous battle in which Florence had defeated Milan. Neither artist finished

Above: Leonardo's **Mona Lisa** *(1503–1506). Although the identity of the lady is unknown, her intriguing expression—the way she looks out of the picture with a mysterious smile—has made the picture one of the most famous in the history of art.*

Right: Leonardo's **The Virgin and Child with Saint Anne** *(about 1508). The Virgin Mary is shown sitting on the lap of her mother, Saint Anne, and reaching down to pick up the baby Jesus. Jesus plays with a lamb, an animal used by artists to symbolize his future suffering.*

the project, although Leonardo made some powerful sketches of men and horses entwined in combat.

In 1506 Leonardo left Florence again and returned to Milan, where he entered the service of the French governor, Charles d'Amboise. The French king, Louis XII, gave him a generous salary as well as ordering new works. In 1507 Charles d'Amboise gave him the task of overseeing the festivities that were arranged to mark Louis's official visit to the city. To the delight of the court Leonardo constructed a walking mechanical lion to greet the king.

Leonardo's most important work from his second stay in Milan is *The*

Virgin and Child with Saint Anne (about 1508), a subject he had tackled several times before. In this painting Leonardo perfected the technique that characterizes his style: "sfumato." This Italian word means "misty" and describes the way in which Leonardo delicately blended areas of light and shade in his paintings so that they appear to merge into each other with no distinct outlines. The technique can be seen in the landscape behind the figures, where the gray, craggy mountains appear to melt into the sky. Sfumato imparts a mysterious, otherworldly glow to Leonardo's paintings.

OLD AGE: ROME AND AMBOISE

In 1512 the French were driven from Milan, and the elderly Leonardo was once again without a home. At first he went to Rome, where he was given rooms at the Vatican. There he devoted himself to his scientific researches, although the pope forbade him to carry out any dissection of human corpses. Although Leonardo was a respected figure, to many people his work seemed old-fashioned or eccentric compared to the achievements of Michelangelo and Raphael. Only one work survives from this time, a somber and mysterious depiction of John the Baptist. It was probably his last painting.

In 1516 Leonardo moved again. The new French king, Francis I (reigned 1515–1547), had long been an admirer of Leonardo's work and now invited him to come to France. Leonardo settled with his pupil and friend Francesco Melzi at a small country house near Amboise. There Leonardo lived in virtual retirement, delighting the king with his learning and making a few designs for buildings.

In May 1518, after a period of illness, Leonardo died and was buried in the cathedral at Amboise. Melzi wrote to inform Leonardo's step-brothers of his death. "Everyone," he wrote, "has been struck by grief because of the loss of such a man, the like of whom it is not in the power of nature to bring forth again."

LEONARDO'S DREAM OF FLIGHT

Many Renaissance engineers tackled the problem of human flight, although none did so successfully. Leonardo was no exception, and many of the designs in his notebooks are for flying machines. Inspired by his studies of birds in flight, Leonardo made sketches for a kind of primitive plane. It had large, flappable wings that were operated by the pilot using a system of ropes and pulleys. His other ideas for flying machines included a kind of a parachute, a glider, and a "helicopter," which was based on a rotating screw. However, with only wood and leather at his disposal Leonardo was never able to develop a machine light enough to get off the ground.

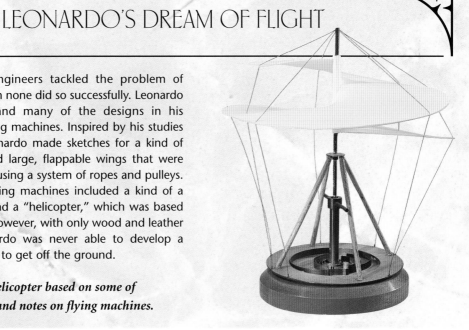

Right: A model of a helicopter based on some of Leonardo's drawings and notes on flying machines.

Literacy

Above: This illustration from a 15th-century French manuscript shows pupils reading from books in a lesson. Before the invention of the printing press, books were precious objects, and only rich people could afford to own them.

Throughout the Renaissance a growing number of people were literate, or able to read and write. Rising levels of literacy were closely connected to the invention and development of printing and to improved, more widely available education. Increased rates of literacy are evident in signed legal documents, personal correspondence, and a huge increase in popular printed texts, from books about the lives of the saints to almanacs and guides to household management.

If literacy is judged by a person's ability to sign his or her name (rather than using a cross or thumb print), then the proportion of the population that was literate remained largely the same as it was in the Middle Ages. However, judged by more advanced criteria, such as the ability to read and write freely, and to understand and evaluate information, the rate of literacy greatly increased in the Renaissance.

Rates of literacy varied widely according to people's social positions, jobs, and whether they lived in the town or countryside. They also varied greatly between men and women. Unlike men, very few women occupied positions or jobs that required them to be able to read and write. If girls received any education, it was usually in how to run a household.

LITERATE NOBILITY

Members of the nobility, who had come to accept that education was a prime requirement for advancement at court, were increasingly literate, as were professionals such as clerics, merchants, physicians, lawyers, and bankers. Increasing state business also fueled demand for educated civil servants. Literacy rates in towns and cities were reasonably high; by the mid-16th century half of Londoners could read and write. Among skilled craftsmen such as goldsmiths and drapers the figure was even higher, probably 50 to 75 percent. The reason for high rates of literacy among craftsmen was that many guilds insisted that boys be able to read and write before they became apprentices.

In rural areas, however, it was a different story. Shepherds, laborers, agricultural workers, and fishermen were, on the whole, illiterate. Unlike their urban counterparts, their work did not require them to be able to read and write. Few received any education. If they did, it was usually from the village priest, who taught them the rudiments of reading. Nevertheless, most villages would have at least one inhabitant who was able to read aloud to the community. The literacy rate of men in 17th-century Scotland, for instance, is estimated at about 25 percent—the low figure probably reflects a rural society.

REVOLUTIONARY CHANGES

Literacy was connected to fundamental transformations in society. Growing economic prosperity led to the founding of schools and colleges. Printing technology also brought revolutionary changes. For the first time books were widely available to the general public. An increasing number of these works were printed in vernacular (local) languages, such as French, English, and German, rather than in Latin, the language of the church, scholars, government, and business. This encouraged lay (non-church) people to read more widely. Books and pamphlets also became cheaper, and more people could afford them—previously only the rich had owned expensive handwritten books. Book-shops were established in towns, and traveling peddlers sold popular titles such as accounts of saints' lives, books of news, and almanacs. It has been estimated that the library of an average physician in the Spanish city of Valencia increased from 26 books at the end of the 15th century to 62 in 1550.

A firm belief of Protestantism was that every individual should be able to read the Bible for himself and discover its meaning. Martin Luther had greatly increased the accessibility of the Bible by translating it into German, and other translations soon followed. An increasing number of Protestant schools opened, even in rural areas, with the intention of making education available to everyone.

SEE ALSO

♦ Biblical Studies
♦ Books and Libraries
♦ Education
♦ Language
♦ Printing

Below: An engraving showing Johannes Gutenberg with the printing press he built in 1436. Printing multiplied the number of books and cut their cost, stimulating literacy.

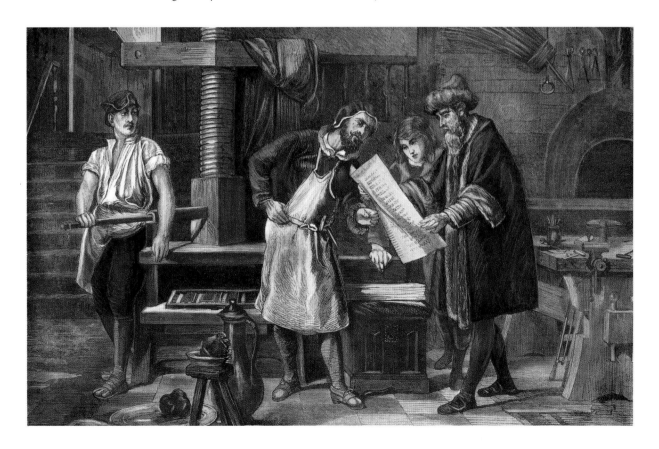

Literature

The writing, printing, and reading of books flourished during the Renaissance. Writers of popular literature started to abandon the scholarly language of Latin and write in the local, or vernacular, language so that their works could be understood by ordinary people. Due to the advent of printing in the early 15th century many more books became available, and many more people were able to read them. Traveling chapmen, or peddlers, hawked "chapbooks"—small books containing ballads, plays, or religious tracts—around towns and villages, where they were often read out loud. Noblemen set up book-lined studies in their homes, and important cities established well-stocked libraries where scholars and citizens could read and consult books.

In this climate a vigorous written literature developed. Writers were able to address a much wider and more varied readership than ever before, and the spread of literature was encouraged by humanist scholars, who believed in the importance of education and study. The humanists held up classical (ancient Greek and Roman) writers as models of what Renaissance writers could achieve. They also believed that the best literature should not only entertain the reader, but also help him or her live a better, more moral life.

Many writers in Italy and later throughout Europe were in accord with humanist ideals. They looked to the ancient writers for inspiration, and

their work contains many references to the mythology, history, philosophy, and literature of ancient Greece and Rome. Renaissance writers also revived some of the forms and themes of classical literature. For example, the Portuguese writer Luis de Camões (about 1524–1580) wrote a long heroic poem that was closely modeled on ancient epic poems such as *The Odyssey* and *The Aeneid*. His work *The Lusiads*, published in 1572, celebrates the achievements of the Portuguese explorer Vasco de Gama (about 1460–1524). The story includes the classical gods Venus and Bacchus, who either

Above: A 16th-century miniature portrait of Luis de Camões, the Portuguese poet who wrote The Lusiads, *a long heroic poem based on classical models. The work of many other Renaissance writers was inspired by the literature of ancient Greece and Rome.*

hamper or help da Gama in his voyage across the Indian Ocean. In England the courtier and poet Edmund Spenser (1554–1586) wrote the epic poem *The Faerie Queen* to glorify England and its queen, Elizabeth I.

THE PASTORAL ROMANCE

Another form of literature popular in the Renaissance was the pastoral romance, inspired by the works of Virgil and the ancient Greek poet Theocritus. Pastoral romances told tales of shepherds and shepherdesses in an idyllic countryside, far from the problems and corruption of city life. The English courtier Sir Philip Sidney wrote one such pastoral, called *Arcadia* (1590), and another pastoral romance called *Rosalynde* (1590) by Sir Thomas Lodge provided Shakespeare with the inspiration for his play *As You Like It.*

The Bible was also a very powerful influence on Renaissance writing. This was especially true in northern Europe, where the leaders of the Reformation believed that everyone should be able to read and study the Old and New Testaments for themselves. So Protestant scholars translated the Bible into

---

The Bible was a powerful influence on Renaissance writing

---

local languages, and these translations had a profound effect on the development of literary language.

In Germany, for example, Martin Luther (1483–1546) produced the first

Below: **The Arcadian Shepherds,** *a painting by Nicolas Poussin (1594–1665). The idea of an idealized life in the countryside had originated in classical times, and it became a popular theme in Renaissance literature. Another common theme was that death is ever-present—here it is symbolized by the tomb in the center of the picture.*

LITERATURE AND THE "NEW WORLD"

The discovery of the Americas at the end of the 15th century had a huge impact on Renaissance literature. The idea of a great unknown land far away across the ocean captured the European imagination, and people read with wonder the accounts of voyages to the Americas, such as Girolamo Benzoni's *Historia del mondo nova* ("History of the New World"), published in Venice in 1565. Many writers thought of the native inhabitants as innocent savages, whose simple ways contrasted with the corruption of the Europeans. In an essay called "On Cannibals," for instance, Montaigne described the Americas as a kind of paradise in which people lived in blissful harmony with nature. And Shakespeare's *The Tempest* (about 1611) may well have been a response to the discovery of the New World—in the play a party of Europeans is shipwrecked on the shores of a strange island inhabited by an enchanter and his slave, the savage Caliban.

Right: The title page of a travel book about the New World by Theodor de Bry (1528–1598). The text was based on Girolamo Benzoni's History of the New World.

translation of the Bible into German and in so doing laid the foundations of modern written German. In England William Tyndale (about 1494–1536) translated the New Testament and part of the Old Testament into English, and the powerful, poetic language he forged helped shape the language of William Shakespeare and his contemporaries in the later 16th century.

STORIES LIKE NOVELS

Renaissance writers also created bold and original works, developing new forms and exploring new themes. One new form was something resembling the modern novel—a long prose narrative dealing with everyday characters in a realistic setting. *La Celestina* (1499), which was probably written by the Spanish Jewish lawyer Fernando de Rojas (about 1465–1541), is sometimes called the first European novel. It tells the story of two young lovers and a woman called La Celestina who acts as a go-between.

Rojas's interest in the workings of his characters' minds matched a wider interest in the individual's psychology in the Renaissance. In France, for example, the *Essays* of Michel de Montaigne (1533–1592) were partly a kind of autobiography—a form that had only rarely been attempted before in literature. In the preface to the *Essays* Montaigne declared: "Here I want to be seen in my simple, natural everyday fashion . . . for it is my own self I am painting." In Poland Jan Kochanowski (1530–1584) explored his grief at the death of his baby daughter in a series of deeply moving poems called *Laments* (1580). And in plays such as his tragedy *Hamlet* (1600) Shakespeare created complex, "rounded" characters quite unlike anything found in earlier plays.

London

The busy trading port of London became England's largest city during the Middle Ages. In the 15th and 16th centuries it continued to grow in area and population, becoming one of the most important cities in Europe.

London was founded beside the Thames River by invading Romans in 43 A.D. Originally the town occupied an area to the east of the center of present-day London. Today this district is still known as "the City" and is London's main financial center. A mile or so to the west of this area an important religious center grew up at Westminster. During the reign of Edward the Confessor in the 11th century it became the site of both a royal palace and an abbey.

London grew steadily over the centuries despite its population being ravaged at various times by fire, famine, and disease. By the end of the 14th century it was both the home of government and an important trading center. Vessels arrived from all over Europe. Venetian galleys sailed regularly from the Mediterranean, docking in London to unload their precious cargo of spices and cloth. They stayed for weeks at one of the quays, such as Billingsgate or Queenhithe, while the merchants sold their goods and then loaded a cargo of English wool, hides, and tin.

Like their equivalents in other major European cities, the merchants and craftsmen of London organized themselves into associations known as guilds. The guilds were extremely

Above: This picture shows the coronation procession of Edward VI in 1537. It is passing through Cheapside, a London street that was one of the city's most important trading areas.

powerful and were heavily involved in the day-to-day running of the city. Each London trade and craft guild had its own meeting hall, and a central Guildhall was completed around 1425. Merchants sold their wares in the great market at Cheapside, where side streets were named after a trade, such as Bread Street and Milk Street.

TUDOR LONDON

London continued to expand in the 16th century. During this period a number of imposing new churches and palaces were built for Henry VII (ruled 1485–1509) and his son Henry VIII (ruled 1509–1547). One of Henry VII's greatest legacies to the city was the creation of a spectacular chapel at Westminster Abbey. Among the several palaces built in and around the city for Henry VIII were Hampton Court and Whitehall, which replaced Westminster as the official royal residence.

One of the key events in Henry VIII's reign was the dissolution of the monasteries, in which the king seized the property of the church. This process had an important effect on London as buildings that had belonged to the church for centuries were quickly sold and converted to private use. The

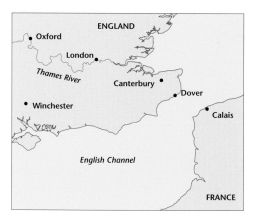

Left: This map shows the position of London on the Thames River in the southeast of England. London was a flourishing port in Renaissance times, carrying on trade with many European cities.

period also saw many noblemen building residential houses between the City and Westminster, joining the two areas for the first time.

During the reign of Elizabeth I (ruled 1558–1603) the population of London grew rapidly. Between 1530 and 1600 it tripled in size to over 200,000. By then London merchants controlled well over half of England's cloth and wool trade, bringing more wealth to their city. As well as being an important trading center, London grew as a base for manufacture as glassworks and dockyards were established outside the city walls. London was also an important cultural center. It was home to the Rose and Globe theaters, which put on plays by writers such as William Shakespeare and Christopher Marlowe.

HENRY VII'S CHAPEL

The building of the present Westminster Abbey was begun in 1245 under King Henry III. At the beginning of the 16th century the abbey's original chapel was pulled down. Henry VII wanted a new chapel as a memorial to himself and his queen, Elizabeth of York, and building began in 1503. The finishing touch to the new chapel was provided by the Florentine sculptor Pietro Torrigiano (1472–1528), who had trained with Michelangelo. Torrigiano came to England around 1511 and over the next few years completed a black marble tomb for Henry and Elizabeth, with gilt bronze effigies of the royal couple. The beautiful decoration around the tomb introduced an Italian Renaissance style to England.

SEE ALSO

♦ England
♦ Guilds and Crafts
♦ Henry VIII
♦ Merchants
♦ Shakespeare
♦ Trade

Luther

Martin Luther (1483–1546) was a key figure in the history of 16th-century Europe. He was the most important leader of the movement known as the Reformation and the founder of the Protestant religion.

Martin Luther was born at Eisleben in Saxony, Germany. His father Hans wanted his son to have a career in law. At the age of 17 Luther enrolled at the University of Erfurt, where he gained an arts degree. In 1505 he went on to study law, but later that year he sold most of his legal books and entered an Augustinian monastery in Erfurt. This was a sudden decision, which came as a shock to his parents.

Luther was made a Roman Catholic priest in 1507, and the following year he went on to Wittenberg University, where he studied theology (religious thought). In 1510 he was one of two monks chosen to travel to Rome to heal a division within the Augustinian brotherhood. He was disappointed by what he saw there. Luther felt that Roman clergymen were more concerned with worldly wealth and power than with important religious matters. On his return to Wittenberg he gained a doctor's degree and in 1512 became professor of biblical theology at the university, a position he held for life.

JUSTIFICATION BY FAITH

By the age of 30 Luther was preaching in his monastery and the local church. At the university he gave lectures on the Bible and devoted his private study to the Epistles of Saint Paul in the New Testament. Luther thought more and more about the meaning of Christian salvation. He came to believe that people find favor with God simply by their faith in his promise that Christ died for their sins. He was convinced that God gave this faith to people as a gift, and that it led people to lead good lives and do good works. This view became known as "justification by

Below: A portrait of Martin Luther by his contemporary Lucas Cranach the Elder. Luther is wearing the simple black robes of the Augustinian religious order.

Right: This illustration from a Protestant pamphlet shows the monk Johann Tetzel selling indulgences in a German town. Luther's attack on the sale of indulgences was central to his dispute with the church.

faith." It was different from the accepted Roman Catholic doctrine, which stated that believers earn favor with God by doing good works.

Luther also disagreed with the Roman Catholic church over the question of indulgences, letters that people could buy from the church that were believed to release them from suffering for their sins. Indulgences were sold by representatives of the pope, but Luther argued that forgiveness could not be bought or even earned, since it was a gift from God. In 1515 Pope Leo X authorized Archbishop Albrecht of Mainz to sell indulgences in order to raise money to help pay for the building of Saint Peter's basilica (church) in Rome. The archbishop appointed a Dominican monk, Johann Tetzel, to collect the money, which he did with great relish. Luther disagreed with the whole business and felt that he had to act. He did so by writing and publishing his famous 95 theses (articles).

When Tetzel wrote countertheses opposing Luther's opinions, the debate was seen by some as simply a disagreement between Augustinian and Dominican monks. However, the disagreement widened when Luther

LUTHER'S PROTEST

Martin Luther's 95 theses were really opinions that were intended as points for discussion. He wrote them with the intention of helping people find their way to the truth, and he sent copies to the archbishop of Mainz, as well as to his bishop. It is traditionally believed that Luther also pinned a copy to the door of the castle church in Wittenberg on October 31, 1517, the eve of All Saints' Day. Further copies were printed and circulated, and the archbishop forwarded one to Rome. The pope decided to ask the head of the Augustinian monks to deal with the matter, and he simply relieved Luther of his duties as a district vicar.

went to Leipzig to debate the issue with a famous theological scholar, Johann Eck. Eck forced Luther to question the authority of church councils, which were held to determine Catholic doctrine (the beliefs taught by the church). Such questioning amounted to an attack on the whole of the church, as well as the pope as its head, something Luther emphasized in his writings of 1520. He stated that all Christians were equal, and that members of the clergy should be subject to the same laws and pay the same taxes as other people. By now the Augustinian monk was pushing the pope too far. Luther's writings were burned in Rome, and in January 1521 Pope Leo X excommunicated him, or expelled him from the church. In April the same year the Holy Roman emperor Charles V also condemned Luther at the Diet of Worms.

LUTHER IN HIDING

Luther's supporters, who included many German princes, took him from Worms and hid him in Wartburg Castle, near Eisenach. Luther stayed there for eight months, spending his time translating the New Testament into German. During his absence from

Left: This painting of Martin Luther preaching and taking communion comes from a 16th-century Danish altar front. Luther's beliefs quickly became popular across northern Europe.

THE DIET OF WORMS

The Diet of Worms was an imperial assembly held in the German town of Worms, on the Rhine River. In April 1521 Martin Luther was called to the assembly to be heard by the young Holy Roman emperor Charles V. When Luther was asked to admit that he had been wrong and to disown his writings, he first asked for some time to think. Next day he stated clearly that he was bound by the Scriptures and could not go against his conscience, and this meant that he could not retract any of his statements. He is traditionally quoted as saying, "Here I stand. I cannot do otherwise." At that the emperor called the meeting to a halt. Shortly afterward Luther was declared an outlaw, and his writings were banned.

Right: The title page of the first German version of the Bible, which was published in 1534. The translation was made by Luther and his colleagues at Wittenberg University.

Wittenberg, however, others in the reform movement were becoming much more forceful, and even violent. Social and religious issues were becoming increasingly intertwined. Luther opposed this development.

Although his religious views were revolutionary, Luther was politically very conservative. He went back to Wittenberg to give a series of powerful sermons in which he condemned the fanatics as well as Catholics. By doing so, he lost some popular support. He went on to oppose the Peasants' Revolt of 1525, writing a political pamphlet entitled "Against the Murdering and Thieving Hoards of Peasants."

Luther never wanted to split the church, only to reform it and make it less corrupt. Nevertheless, a split is what his ideas brought about. In 1530 Luther's fellow reformer Philipp Melanchthon wrote a summary of Lutheran beliefs that was presented to Emperor Charles V. This summary, called the Augsburg Confession, pointed out the similarities between Lutheran and Catholic beliefs, but by then the Reformation was making its way across northern Europe.

FINAL YEARS

Luther continued to lecture at Wittenberg University, and in 1534 he and his colleagues completed their translation of the Old Testament into German. He also wrote a number of hymns and translated others from Latin. With the Reformation in full swing Luther was asked in 1546 to help settle a disagreement between two young princes. He traveled through the snow to Eisleben and settled the quarrel, but the next day he died. His body was taken to Wittenberg, where he was buried in the Church of All Saints.

Machiavelli

An Italian statesman and writer, Niccolò Machiavelli (1469–1527) wrote a famous work on the politics of power entitled *The Prince*. Machiavelli used his experience of Florentine politics to outline the qualities needed by a successful politician. Those qualities included ruthlessness and the use of cruelty and violence to achieve goals—the term "Machiavellian" is used today to describe a schemer and manipulator. Machiavelli's theoretical approach to politics was startling and new, and he has been called the father of modern political science.

Machiavelli was born in Florence, the son of a not very successful lawyer. The young Niccolò went to school, where he learned Latin, but much of his education came from the books he found in his own home. This self-motivated study helped him think for himself; and as he grew up, he developed original ideas. He gained a position in the Florentine government and in 1498 became second chancellor, which was a very important administrative role. That gave him the opportunity to travel on diplomatic missions for Florence. His first important journey was to the French court in 1500. The following year, aged 32, he married Marietta Corsini, with whom he had five children.

THE CITY-STATE OF FLORENCE

At the beginning of the 16th century there was great rivalry between Florence and other Italian city-states.

The Florentine republic was also in conflict with the pope, the Holy Roman emperor, and the kings of France and Spain. Machiavelli was convinced that Florence needed its own militia, or military force raised from the citizens of the state. This was a new idea; Italian city-states traditionally hired mercenary troops—who would fight for whoever paid them—when they were needed. Machiavelli convinced the chief magistrate of the city, however, and the Florentine militia was set up in

Above: A 16th-century portrait of Machiavelli from the Uffizi Gallery in Florence. Machiavelli's experience of the cutthroat nature of political life in Renaissance Italy informed his writings on politics and history.

THE PRINCE

In *The Prince* Machiavelli described the ways in which a ruler (or "prince") could gain and keep power. A ruler must be strong in order to run an ordered, balanced state, he wrote, and must be prepared to use force and even cruelty if necessary. He must combine the cunning of a fox with the strength of a lion. The ruler must have a powerful army, since his power can only be preserved by using the threat of force. In order to create a healthy state, ruthless means are justified, even if they involve deceit or murder. Machiavelli wrote that a prince's personal morality is a luxury that must be set aside in the interests of the state.

Machiavelli dedicated the book to Lorenzo de Medici in an attempt to gain the favor of the Medici and regain a government position. However, the character of Machiavelli's ideal prince himself is commonly supposed to have been inspired by Cesare Borgia (1475–1507), a ruthless politician and military leader. Machiavelli, in fact, hated Borgia as a man, but still admired the cunning, unscrupulous way in which he exercised power.

Right: The frontispiece of Machiavelli's best-known work, **The Prince.** *Many people believed that Machiavelli was parodying ruthless leaders in his book, but his admiration was sincere.*

NICOLAI
MACHIAVELLI
PRINCEPS.

EX
SYLVESTRI TELII
FVLGINATIS TRADVCTIONE
diligenter emendata.

Adiecta sunt eiusdem argumenti, Aliorum quorundam contra Machiauelium scripta de potestate & officio Principum, & contra tyrannos.

BASILEAE
Ex officina Petri Pernae.
M D XXC.

1506. Machiavelli was then made secretary of the council that controlled the militia.

Machiavelli met many important people on his diplomatic travels, including Pope Julius II, the Holy Roman emperor Maximilian I, and King Louis XII of France. These meetings convinced him that Florence would soon be caught up in a major war. Before this could happen, however, the republic was overthrown—in 1512, backed by papal and Spanish armies, the Medici family returned to their former power in Florence. Machiavelli was dismissed and soon accused of plotting against Giovanni de Medici, who the following year was to become Pope Leo X. Machiavelli was thrown into prison; but even under torture he protested his innocence, and less than a year later he

was released. In 1513 he retired to the property near Florence that he had inherited from his father, and there he wrote *The Prince*, which was published in 1532, five years after his death, and immediately attracted condemnation.

FRUSTRATED AMBITION

During his retirement Machiavelli always hoped to return to active politics but never achieved his goal. In 1520 the University of Florence appointed him official historiographer (writer of history) of the republic, and in 1526 he became secretary of a committee that controlled Florentine fortifications. When the Medici were thrown out of power a year later, he had hopes of a political appointment, but the new leaders of the republic ignored him. The disappointed Machiavelli died shortly afterward.

Magic and Superstition

Left: An early 17th-century painting entitled The Fortuneteller. *Fortunetellers in the Renaissance used a variety of methods to foretell a person's future. They included gazing into a crystal ball, dealing out Tarot (fortune-telling) cards, throwing dice, and reading the lines on a person's palm. One of the best-known ways of looking into the future was through astrology, which was a highly respected science that was taught at universities.*

In the 15th and 16th centuries most people believed in magic and superstition. Magic was understood to be the use of supernatural powers to make impossible things happen, while superstition was believing that certain events could herald good or bad fortune.

People wanted to believe in powers that could help them cope with the harsh reality of daily life, such as bad weather, crop failure, or sickness in their animals. Between the 15th and 17th centuries fortunetellers, healers, and wise men and women were common throughout Europe, and most ordinary people imagined that the countryside was full of good and bad spirits.

Often the line between Christian and non-Christian belief was blurred. Both Christianity and pagan beliefs demanded faith in unknown forces. Wearing a magical amulet around one's neck or keeping a copy of the Lord's Prayer in one's shoe both served to protect the wearer from harm. Belief in magic was reinforced by the church's numerous stories of miracles, visions, and exorcisms—forcing evil spirits to leave a person's "possessed" body—which were taken as evidence of God's power on earth. Saints featured heavily in the popular imagination; and their relics, which might be a piece of bone, a fingernail, or a hair, were believed to hold magical properties that would bring good fortune and cure illness.

THE WITCHES' HAMMER

The church's attitude to witchcraft hardened toward the end of the 15th century. In 1484 Pope Innocent VIII issued a papal bull (a decree) condemning the spread of witchcraft in Germany and authorizing two inquisitors, Heinrich Kraemer and Jacob Sprenger, to wipe it out. Two years later Kraemer and Sprenger published their *Malleus Maleficarum* ("The Witches' Hammer"), a handbook describing how to hunt down and interrogate suspected witches.

The book was divided into three parts. Part one was concerned with affirming the reality of witches—any disbelief was condemned as heresy—while part two was a collection of lurid tales of witches'

satanic activities. Part three discussed the legal procedures to be followed in witch trials, including a detailed description of the use of torture to extract a confession.

The *Malleus Maleficarum* claimed that witches could transform themselves into any form—usually that of a cat. They flew naked on broomsticks and attended nighttime gatherings, known as "Witches' Sabbaths," at which they feasted on dead babies, had sex with the devil, and performed the Black Mass, which was a parody of the Communion service. The book explained the large number of female witches by maintaining that women were particularly vulnerable to the temptations of the devil.

Below: An illustration from a 15th-century book on alchemy. It shows alchemists at work preparing experiments to distill various materials in their search for gold.

Outside the church there were two main categories of magic: everyday and hermetic. Everyday magic played a regular part in rural culture. Wise men and women prescribed a potent mix of herbal remedies, rituals, and charms to cure unrequited love, visitations by evil spirits, or a sick cow. While many people feared their powers, their vital role in the community usually ensured they were protected from persecution during witch hunts of the time.

SECRET MAGIC

Hermetic, or scholarly, magic derived from the mysterious writings of Hermes Trismegistus, which date from the first to the third century A.D., but which were supposedly based on revelations made by the Egyptian god Thoth. Knowledge of this magic, which included alchemy and astrology, was shrouded in secrecy, but was tolerated by the church as part of an ancient mystical tradition that aimed to unlock the secrets of the universe.

Left: **A Witches' Gathering,** *a 17th-century painting showing the popular idea of what went on when witches assembled together at night to feast, cavort with the devil, and hold a Black Mass.*

Alchemy sought to find a substance, called the "philosopher's stone," that could turn any metal into gold and make people immortal. Alchemists were widely regarded as magicians, and popular legend told how one such scholar—Dr. Faustus—sold his soul to the devil in exchange for this secret knowledge. Astrology involved foretelling future events from the movements of the stars and planets, and was taken seriously enough to be taught in universities. It was widely used in everyday life to foresee the future, to choose a lucky date for an important event, or to predict the appearance of bad omens such as shooting stars and eclipses of the sun or moon.

WITCHCRAFT

In addition people believed in witches and witchcraft. Witches were thought to be in league with the devil and to perform evil acts that caused harm to people, property, and crops. The church condemned witchcraft as heresy and was dedicated to rooting it out. At that time the church was weak and divided; it was able to give itself a strong sense of purpose by promoting a fear of the devil and witchcraft.

As a result of the church's attitude widespread persecution of people suspected of witchcraft lasted for 300 years. The witch hunts reached their height between 1580 and 1650 in Germany, France, and Switzerland. It is thought that around 60,000 "witches" were put to death, of whom 80 percent were women. Often single, elderly, or deformed, and from the poorest sections of society, accused witches were a scapegoat (someone who bears the blame for others) for calamitous events such as crop failure.

Torture was used to get confessions; and if the authorities got carried away, entire communities could be wiped out as more and more "witches" were denounced. In 1585, after one such witch hunt in Germany, two villages were left with only two people alive between them. Wichcraft trials continued up until the 18th century, when there was a gradual decline in belief in magic and superstition.

SEE ALSO

♦ Alchemy
♦ Astrology
♦ Inquisition
♦ Medicine and Surgery

Mannerism

Mannerism is a term used to describe a style in art that was popular in Italy between about 1520 and 1600. It comes from the Italian word *maniera*, meaning "manner" or "style," which was used in the mid-16th century to refer to works of art that were considered graceful and sophisticated. Mannerist artists devoted themselves to developing these qualities in their paintings, sculptures, and buildings.

Mannerism developed in the work of a number of artists in Florence and Rome in the second quarter of the 16th century. They included the painters Rosso Fiorentino, Jacopo Pontormo, Bronzino, and Parmigianino; the sculptors Benvenuto Cellini and Giambologna; and the architect Giulio Romano. Although later scholars viewed their work as breaking away from the values of Renaissance art, mannerist artists believed that they were continuing existing traditions.

THE SEEDS OF MANNERISM

Many of the characteristics that are defined as mannerist were already present in the paintings and sculptures of an earlier generation of artists, particularly Raphael (1483–1520) and Michelangelo (1474–1564), who are considered two of the greatest masters of the Renaissance. In particular, mannerist artists drew on the polish and grace—or *maniera*—of Raphael's style and the serene faces of his female figures and angels. They were also inspired by his more emotionally

Left: Giambologna's marble sculpture The Rape of the Sabine Women *(1581–1582). This complex group of twisting figures is carved to be seen from all sides (rather than just the front) and is a supreme display of the artist's skill.*

charged late work, like *The Transfiguration* (begun in 1517). Other mannerist artists were inspired by the powerfully expressive forms of Michelangelo's paintings and sculptures, particularly his muscular figures with exaggerated proportions arranged in complicated poses—such as those in his paintings on the ceiling of the Sistine Chapel in Rome (1508–1512).

FEATURES OF MANNERISM

One characteristic of mannerist art is its "artificial" appearance. Mannerists presented their subjects in a far from lifelike or natural way, with the result that their style is often more striking than the subject matter. In many senses this was a continuation of existing ideas. Ever since the early 15th century artists had not only worked to portray people and objects as they appeared in nature, but had tried to find an "ideal" or perfect beauty that went beyond nature. They believed that this ideal beauty could be seen in classical (ancient Greek and Roman) art.

Mannerist artists also admired classical art. However, many of them moved away from its basic principles of order and harmony that were expressed in balanced compositions (arrangements) and the lifelike proportions of figures. This departure from tradition made mannerism unpopular with some later critics.

GRACE AND ELEGANCE

For many mannerist artists ideal beauty was expressed by depicting the human form with long, slender limbs. They associated these exaggerated proportions with grace and elegance. Parmigianino's (1503–1540) painting the *Madonna and Child with Angels* (about 1535), commonly known as *The Madonna of the Long Neck*, clearly

shows the mannerist taste for elongated proportions. Mary (the Madonna) is painted with a long, slender neck; indeed, her whole body is stretched out right down to her slim fingers. The infant Jesus is also shown with a long, thin body sprawling in a languid pose. Both Mary and the angels have the calm, almond-shaped faces that were popular in mannerist art.

Parmigianino's picture also shows the breaks with Renaissance ideals that many scholars find an unattractive aspect of mannerism. For example, the composition of the picture lacks

Above: **The Madonna of the Long Neck,** *painted by Parmigianino in about 1535. Its elongated figures are a typical feature of mannerist art.*

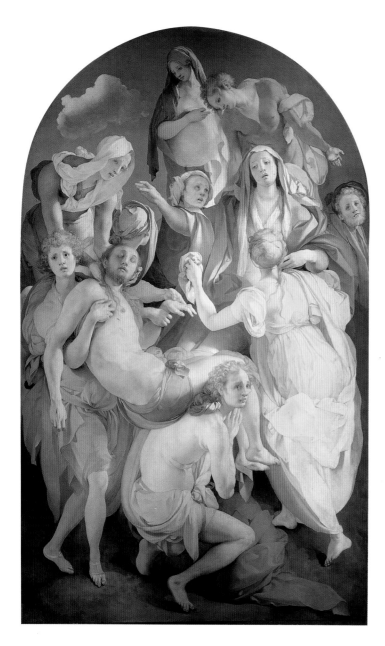

Above: Pontormo's **Deposition** *(about 1528). Acid colors and strong lighting like those seen here typify mannerism.*

One aspect of the artifice (artificial appearance) of mannerism was an emphasis on the skill of the artist, which often took the form of a highly polished style. For example, the painter Bronzino produced pictures with a very smooth finish. The faces, hands, and nude bodies in his portraits and famous allegory of love, *Venus, Cupid, Time, and Folly* (1545), are so smoothly painted that they look like porcelain. Similarly, the work of the goldsmith and sculptor Benvenuto Cellini (1500–1571) was extremely refined in its technique. In a famous gold saltcellar that he made for Francis I of France he brought the precious materials, meticulous approach, and polished finish of jewelry to sculpture.

COMPLEX POSES

Artists like Cellini also displayed their skill by portraying the human form in very complicated poses. Again there was nothing new in this tendency. Renaissance painters and sculptors had long displayed their mastery by representing the nude body. Inspired by classical sculptures like *The Laocoön*, which shows a muscular man writhing to escape from serpents, Michelangelo excelled at sculpting and painting bodies twisting in a corkscrewlike pose known as a *figura serpenta*.

One mannerist in particular, the sculptor Giambologna, developed this complex pose, and in his work it practically became an end in itself. Like Cellini, he was a master at creating graceful, elegant sculptures that belied the heaviness of the materials from which they were made. In his marble group of three interlocked figures *The Rape of the Sabine Women* (1581–1582, see page 30) he conveys a sense of drama and energetic movement as a woman is carried off (here "rape"

balance and order. Rather than being arranged symmetrically around the Madonna and Child, the angels are bunched into the left-hand side of the picture. Also, while earlier Renaissance artists had worked hard to present a lifelike sense of space in their pictures, the mannerists played with their portrayal of space and scale. At the bottom right of Parmigianino's picture, for example, there is a tiny figure of a prophet that looks impossibly small compared to the Madonna.

MANNERIST ARCHITECTURE

In architecture mannerism was typically expressed by deliberately breaking established rules. Earlier in the Renaissance architects such as Brunelleschi and Bramante had studied classical (ancient Greek and Roman) architecture and developed guidelines to determine how classical elements, such as columns, should be used. The mannerists intentionally turned these rules on their head. One of the earliest mannerist buildings is the Palazzo del Tè in Mantua (begun 1526), designed by Giulio Romano, who had been Raphael's chief assistant. There classical details are willfully misused so that some stones appear to have slipped out of place. Michelangelo also played with the rules of classical architecture in a building he designed at about the same time: the entrance hall and stairway to the Laurentian Library (begun 1524). The curved stairs seem to pour out of the library, while columns are sunk into the walls and set above large brackets—traditionally columns stood out and carried the weight of the ceiling. Elsewhere mannerist architects adopted an even more playful approach, as in the Palazzo Zuccari (1591) in Rome, designed by the painter and architect Federico Zuccari, where the windows and doors are designed to look like open mouths.

Right: A face-shaped window from the Palazzo Zuccari in Rome (1591), one of the most light-hearted examples of mannerism.

means abduction). The woman and two men in the sculpture are arranged to form a supple spiral rising like a corkscrew from the base up to the woman's outstretched hand at the top.

UNNATURAL COLORS

In painting mannerist artists often used unnatural, almost harsh colors, which they enhanced by combining them with areas of strong light and shade. These features can be seen in Pontormo's *Deposition* (about 1528), which shows Christ's body after it has been taken down from the cross. His body (based on Michelangelo's sculpture the *Pietà*) is bleached out, as if a bright light is being shone on it, and the acid pinks, blues, and greens of the mourners' clothes are set off by patches

of brilliant orange. The faces are stricken with grief and anxiety. The proportions of the bodies and the poses are exaggerated, especially the crouching figure who bears Christ's weight at the bottom.

It is these qualities, the elongated proportions, complex poses, sweet faces, and bright colors, that characterize art from the mannerist period. The fashion for this "mannered" style soon spread from the Italian cities where it had developed to other parts of Europe, particularly the courts of the French king Francis I at Fontainebleau and the Holy Roman emperor Rudolf II in Prague. However, in Italy itself, by the end of the 16th century mannerism was eclipsed by another more dramatic and monumental style: the baroque.

SEE ALSO
♦ Architecture
♦ Baroque
♦ Bronzino
♦ Cellini
♦ Classicism
♦ Francis I
♦ Giambologna
♦ Michelangelo
♦ Painting
♦ Raphael
♦ Sculpture

Mantegna

Andrea Mantegna (about 1431–1505) was a highly respected painter who spent most of his career working as court artist to the Gonzaga family in Mantua, northern Italy. He was noted particularly for his keen interest in antiquity (the art and culture of ancient Greece and Rome) and for his mastery of foreshortening and perspective, two pictorial techniques he used to make his pictures look more lifelike and imposing.

Mantegna was born near Padua, northern Italy, in about 1431, the son of a master carpenter. At around the age of 12 he was apprenticed to the Paduan artist Francesco Squarcione, whose passionate interest in antiquity greatly influenced Mantegna. His style was also shaped by the work of several leading artists from Florence, which he would have seen in Padua or nearby Venice. The most famous of these artists was Donatello, who worked in Padua between 1443 and 1453. Mantegna also had close links with the Bellini family, the leading artists in Venice in the 15th century, and in 1453 he married Nicolosia Bellini, who was the sister of Giovanni Bellini.

By 1448 Mantegna had completed his training and was one of a number of artists working on frescoes (paintings on wet or "fresh" plaster) in the Ovetari Chapel in the Erimitani Church in Padua. His paintings showed scenes from the lives of Saint James and

Left: Mantegna's ceiling in the Camera degli Sposi (1465–1474) at the ducal palace in Mantua. It is painted to look as if the ceiling is open to the sky, with court ladies, putti (winged babies), a peacock, and a man wearing a turban looking down into the room.

Saint Christopher set against classical architecture, such as columns and triumphal arches. He used perspective to create a feeling of space in his pictures and drew the people with great accuracy, often foreshortening them (or compressing the proportions of their bodies) to give them the shapes our eyes would see if we were actually looking at real people.

Mantegna made his name with the Ovetari frescoes and shortly afterward was commissioned to paint a magnificent altarpiece (1459) for the church of San Zeno in the nearby city of Verona. It was also at this time that he came to the attention of Ludovico Gonzaga, whose court in Mantua was a center of humanism, the new learning that characterized the Renaissance. Ludovico saw in Mantegna a painter who was able to give visual form to the humanist interest in classical texts and archaeology, and in 1460 he appointed him court artist.

Above: **Captured Statues and Siege Equipment,** *one of the paintings in Mantegna's series the* **Triumph of Caesar** *(1484–late 1490s). Mantegna knew a great deal about antiquity, and the pictures are packed with classical details.*

SEE ALSO

♦ Antiquities
♦ Bellini, Giovanni
♦ Classicism
♦ Gonzaga Family
♦ Naturalism
♦ Perspective

Mantegna produced his most distinguished work for the Gonzaga family. His first major project for them was a decorative scheme for the walls and ceilings of the Camera degli Sposi ("the wedding chamber") in the ducal palace. Its main theme was the glorification of the Gonzagas, and around the walls Mantegna painted a series of group portraits of the family and their household engaged in various activities. Everything is meticulously and clearly portrayed, from the faces of the courtiers and the patterned fabrics of their clothing to details such as a pet dog sitting under Ludovico's chair, so that the scenes seem to be actually happening in the room. Mantegna painted the center of the ceiling to look as if it were open to the sky, surrounded by a balustrade with people peering over it. Word of these remarkable frescoes spread quickly across Italy, and artists praised the way that Mantegna had created a realistic feeling of space and marveled at his "illusionist" ceiling.

THE TRIUMPH OF CAESAR

In about 1484 Mantegna began work on his second great commission for the Gonzagas, this time probably for Francesco II. It was a series of 10 canvases (only nine of which survive) showing the triumphs of the Roman general Julius Caesar. The first eight canvases show Roman soldiers leading a victory procession, waving banners and flaunting the spoils of war, while the ninth picture shows Caesar enthroned on a magnificent chariot. Mantegna based his paintings on classical and contemporary accounts and on his knowledge of antique art and archaeology. His detailed and lively portrayals of these classical scenes are some of the clearest expressions of the Renaissance fascination with antiquity.

Manufacturing

Left: This 16th-century fresco shows cannon barrels being made in an armaments factory. In the Renaissance period large quantities of metal were used in the manufacture of weapons.

Trade and industry flourished in the Renaissance, and manufacturing, the production of goods from raw materials, thrived. It was carried out on a much smaller scale than in the huge factories we are familiar with today, in small workshops, forges, kilns, and mills. Common manufactured products included cloth and metal and leather goods, as well as luxuries such as glassware and ceramics.

Most of the products manufactured during the Renaissance had been made in Europe for many centuries, but by the 15th century many more people were able to afford them. The population was growing, creating a larger potential market. More people lived in towns and cities, and so could more easily buy the products available as well as providing the labor to make them. Above all, many peoples' incomes were rising, which meant they had money to spend on items other than essentials such as food. Busy overland trade routes and international trade fairs also meant that goods could be transported quickly and cheaply.

KINDS OF MANUFACTURING

Cloth was the most important kind of manufacturing in both medieval and Renaissance times, and was the staple of Europe's traditional manufacturing heartlands—Flanders (a region that included present-day Belgium and parts of the Netherlands and France) and central and northern Italy. Cities and regions often specialized in a particular kind of textile. In Italy Florence was renowned for its fine woolens, and Naples was known for its silk. The French capital Paris excelled in the making of luxurious tapestries, while rural Normandy made cheap woolens. English weavers produced an expensive kind of thick woolen fabric called broadcloth.

Cloth manufacturing was widespread in Europe because the raw materials (the wool, cotton, and silk) were extremely easy to transport, the manufacturing process simple, and demand high. Many other industries, however, tended to be sited close to sources of raw materials and energy—water, coal, or charcoal.

METALWORKING

Proximity to a source of power was particularly important in metalworking industries. The iron industry expanded around 1500 as new technology developed to make both the mining and smelting (extraction of metal from ore, the stone in which it is found) more efficient. Huge mechanical hammers were used to break up the ore, and large bellows blasted hot air through furnaces to melt the ore and create cast iron. All this machinery was driven by waterpower, and so blast furnaces were located near fast-running rivers. The iron they produced was sold to smaller forges and workshops, where blacksmiths made it into tools, nails, horseshoes, plows, and chains, and armorers crafted it into armor and weapons.

Other sorts of manufacturing industries satisfied demand for food and drink. Commercial brewing flourished in the towns of Germany, Flanders, and Holland from the 14th century. In the 16th century the Dutch also began to dominate the lucrative market for pickled and salted herring. They developed large boats called *buizen* or busses, which were like floating factories where the fish were

Left: This illustration shows an official in a 16th-century metalworks testing a piece of bronze. The metalworking industry saw a huge growth in the 16th century as new techniques made the extraction of metal easier.

both caught and salted, ready for distribution. In southern Europe the production of wine and olive oil were important industries. Sugar refineries opened up in Sicily and Spain, often employing as many as 40 or 50 people, a sizable workforce for the time.

Other kinds of manufacturing concentrated on producing luxury goods, and many cities became associated with a particular kind of product. For example, Venice was celebrated for its glass, Faenza in northern Italy for its faience (a kind of glazed earthenware pottery), and Brabant (a region on the present-day Dutch–Belgian border) for its fur clothes and bell-casting.

The Renaissance period also saw the manufacture of new kinds of goods using recently developed technology. Printing was the most important of these new industries. Johannes Gutenberg (about 1390–1468) perfected the printing press in 1453. A mere 50 years later there were about 1,000 presses in Europe. The largest was in Antwerp and was run by the French printer Christophe Plantin (about 1520–1589). It employed more than 50 people. The printing industry was supplied with paper made in mills that had grown up in Italy, France, and Germany from the 13th century onward.

THE NATURE OF MANUFACTURING

Manufacturing in Renaissance times was very unlike the mass-production methods used in factories today. Most goods were made on a very small scale—often in a workshop that was attached to a home—and using traditional handicraft skills. The technology used to make the goods had changed little from medieval times. There were lots of people available to work cheaply, and so there was no need for labor-saving devices. In addition, workshops were usually small, and masters often had little money to spend on expensive machinery. The powerful trade associations known as guilds also resisted change, which they feared might threaten the status or prosperity of skilled workers.

Workshops were owned and run by a highly skilled craftsman, called the master, who specialized in a single

> *Workshops were usually owned and run by a highly skilled craftsman called the master*

trade. The master usually had only a handful of employees, often including family members and one or two apprentices. Within a town all the masters of a trade belonged to a guild, an association that laid down strict rules and regulations to protect the interests of the trade.

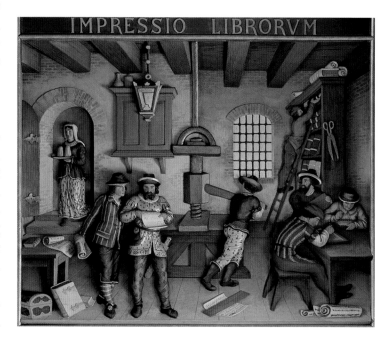

Below: This painted wooden carving shows a printer's workshop in Denmark. After the invention of the printing press in the mid-15th century the printing industry expanded at a rapid rate.

THE ARSENALE

By far the largest manufacturing complex during the Renaissance was the Arsenale, the shipyards of Venice. The Arsenale's name derived from the Arabic word *darsina'a*, meaning "home of industry." Both merchant ships and light, swift-moving naval galleys were vital for Venice's peace and prosperity, and from the 14th century the city government took overall control of the shipyards, turning them into Europe's largest and most advanced industry.

The Arsenale dominated the eastern end of Venice's main island. It was surrounded by mighty walls and could be entered only by two gateways—one from the land and one from the sea. Within the walls was an array of docks, basins, and workshops, where thousands of men labored on making, equipping, and repairing the ships. The workers were highly paid and received many privileges, including free housing.

The Arsenale's production methods were highly efficient and streamlined. Squads of 20 craftsmen and their apprentices worked on different phases of construction, and standardized parts meant that both production and repair were quick and easy. In time of

Above: Shipbuilders at work in the Venice Arsenale. The Arsenale employed thousands of craftsmen.

crisis the Arsenale's output was phenomenal. In 1470, when the Ottoman fleet threatened to seize the Venetian colony of Cyprus, it produced some 100 galleys in two months, more than one a day.

In the 16th century many artisans began to lose their independence as rich businessmen took control of a trade. These entrepreneurs were often merchants who both supplied the raw materials and marketed the finished products. Sometimes, however, they were particularly successful masters who came to dominate the poorer artisans in the same trade. Usually the entrepreneurs "put out" manufacturing work to various artisans working in different places, called "outworkers," and then paid them for their work.

Occasionally, however, these entrepreneurs set up sizable workplaces with a large workforce, enabling them to oversee the work more easily and to streamline the production process. In Segovia in Spain, for example, one textile workshop employed more than a hundred people and included every stage of production from spinning to weaving and finishing.

BOOM AND BUST

Toward the end of the 16th century much of Europe's industry went into a sharp decline. Falling wages and rising prices and taxes meant that people had far less to spend. War and other kinds of social upheaval also took their toll. Italy suffered particularly badly. Other countries were able to adapt to the changes by introducing new technology and production processes or by shifting manufacture out into the countryside, where labor was cheaper. In Italy the powerful guilds often resisted developments such as these. By contrast, the industries of England and Holland flourished.

SEE ALSO

♦ Capitalism
♦ Decorative Arts
♦ Food and Drink
♦ Glass
♦ Guilds and Crafts
♦ Merchants
♦ Mining
♦ Printing
♦ Tapestry
♦ Technology
♦ Textiles
♦ Trade
♦ Transportation
♦ Wealth

Maps and Mapmaking

In the Renaissance there was a major revolution in maps and the art of mapmaking (cartography). Maps became more accurate as a result of the voyages of discovery that took place from the 15th century and improved techniques of cartography. The invention of printing also meant that maps could be produced quickly, cheaply, and in large numbers.

The duke's palace in Genoa, Italy, is home to a map called the planisphere of Paolo dal Pozzo Toscanelli (a planisphere is a type of map). Toscanelli's map was, no doubt, known to the Genoese explorer Christopher Columbus. It is typical of maps produced before Columbus's voyage of discovery in 1492 and shows the world as it was then known, consisting of Europe, Asia, and North Africa. Of North and South America and the vast reaches of the Pacific Ocean there is no trace.

Less than a century later maps such as Gerardus Mercator's world map of 1569 show a startling transformation (see box on page 43). The known world had increased dramatically, with the addition of the Americas and the Pacific Ocean. Maps produced in the 16th century were also overlaid with a grid of lines, called lines of longitude and latitude, that sailors could use to calculate their position. Earlier maps such as Toscanelli's had no such lines.

GREAT ADVANCES IN MAPMAKING

The difference between the two maps shows the great advances in mapmaking that took place during the Renaissance. Late 14th- and 15th-century maps still reflected the medieval view of the world. Most medieval mapmakers were monks, not geographers or explorers, and much of what they showed on maps was based on legend, superstition, and Christian

Left: The 15th-century planisphere of Paolo Toscanelli. It shows North Africa, Europe, and Asia—the extent of the known world at that time.

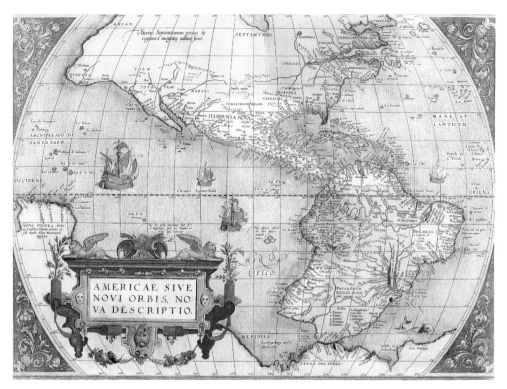

Left: A map of the Americas drawn by Abraham Ortelius in about 1579. Since Columbus made landfall in the West Indies in 1492, Europeans had mapped the coastlines of North and South America and explored much of the interior. However, the west coastline of South America and the position of the southern continent at the bottom of the map are inaccurate.

teaching. Although the ancient Greeks knew that the world is a sphere, much of their knowledge was lost in the Middle Ages. Many medieval mapmakers showed the earth as a flat disk. Arab maps of the same period were more accurate, partly because they drew on the knowledge of ancient Greek geographers such as Ptolemy, who lived in the second century A.D.

PTOLEMY'S *GUIDE*

Ptolemy had compiled a *Guide to Geography* consisting of eight books. It included more than 25 maps and an account of the various forms of projection that Greek cartographers used to represent the curved surface of the earth on flat maps. Greek geographers developed the notions of latitude and longitude, drawing on their maps lines running east–west called "parallels" and north–south called "meridians." They enabled mapmakers to represent features such as coastlines in correct relation to one another.

In western Europe more accurate maps began to be produced again in the 14th century. They were seamen's charts called portolans. Portolans provided information on coastlines, ports, and anchorage points, and gave magnetic compass bearings to help sailors navigate from one place to another. As trade and shipping increased, these sea charts were much in demand. Ship's pilots and captains from different ports often shared their knowledge so that sea charts could be made as accurate as possible.

THE AGE OF DISCOVERY

In the 15th century three advances helped European mapmakers draw more accurate maps and sparked a general interest in cartography. First, Ptolemy's works were translated into Latin, the European language of learning. Second, the introduction of printing in the mid-15th century meant that copies of maps could be produced much more easily and cheaply. For the first time maps became available to a wider range of people, not just princes, scholars, and sailors. Third, the revolution in mapmaking was driven by the new discoveries made on the great voyages of exploration that began in the 15th century.

VOYAGES OF EXPLORATION

The nations principally involved in these voyages, at least in the early days, were Portugal and Spain. From the mid-15th century ships commissioned by the Portuguese prince, Henry "the Navigator," extended the boundaries of the known world by sailing farther and farther south down the west coast of Africa. In 1488 Bartholomeu Dias finally rounded Africa's southern tip to reach the Indian Ocean. Ten years later another Portuguese navigator, Vasco da Gama, sailed across the Indian Ocean

to reach the port of Calicut on the west coast of India.

Meanwhile, the Spanish king and queen Ferdinand and Isabella sponsored the Genoese captain Christopher Columbus to find a sea route to India by sailing westward. In 1492 he sailed across the Atlantic Ocean and discovered the islands now known as the West Indies, territory that he claimed in the name of Spain. On later voyages Columbus reached the coast of South America. Within two years European maps were recording the discovery of the vast South American continent, which Columbus called the Mondo Novo, or "New World."

Columbus embarked on his first voyage armed with maps reflecting Ptolemy's knowledge of geography. Knowing that the earth was round, he sailed westward across the Atlantic with

Left: A 17th-century engraving showing the Flemish mapmakers Gerardus Mercator (left) and Jodocus Hondius (right). Hondius worked in England and Amsterdam, and his maps were some of the first to chart the voyages of the English explorer Francis Drake.

MERCATOR'S PROJECTION

Since before Ptolemy's day mapmakers were aware of the difficulties of representing the curved surface of the globe on flat pieces of paper. Around 1560 Gerardus Mercator devised a new world projection. It was rectangular in shape and divided the world up by using east–west parallels and north–south meridians to show latitude and longitude. One of the aims of Mercator's new projection was to help sailors navigate across the open ocean. Lines drawn between ports on the map yielded compass bearings that seamen could follow to reach their destination. Mercator's projection allows the shape of the world's continents to be shown accurately, but distorts scale, particularly in the far north of the globe. On maps drawn according to this projection northern landmasses such as Greenland appear much bigger than they really are.

In 1569 Mercator produced a famous world map drawn according to his new projection. Now known as Mercator's projection, it remains one of the most

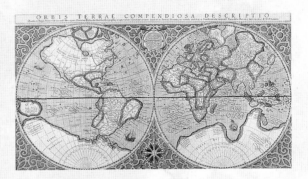

Above: A world map of 1589 based on Mercator's projection. It was made by Mercator's son Rumbold.

familiar ways of representing the world. Later he produced a collection of maps he called an atlas, after the giant in Greek mythology who holds the world on his shoulders. Books of maps have been known as atlases ever since.

the aim of reaching China and the East, rich in spices and silks. Columbus died believing that he had fulfilled his mission and reached Japan and islands off the Chinese coast. However, in 1519 Columbus's view of the world was overturned by the Portuguese captain Ferdinand Magellan. Financed by Spain, Magellan's fleet crossed the Atlantic and rounded the southern tip of South America to find a vast new ocean that Magellan named the Pacific. Three years later, in 1522, a handful of Magellan's original crew limped back to Spain, having completed the first circumnavigation of the world.

A NEW VIEW OF THE WORLD

The discoveries made by explorers were quickly entered on maps that soon reflected a new, enlarged view of the world. In 1500 the map of Columbus's pilot, Juan de la Cosa, was the first to show the discoveries in the New World.

In 1507 the German mapmaker Martin Waldseemüller may have been first to name the new lands "America," in mistaken honor of the Italian navigator Amerigo Vespucci. Waldseemüller later tried to change the name he had chosen, but it had already taken hold.

New techniques in mapmaking paralleled the revolution that was taking place in map content. In this field Flemish cartographers, including Gerardus Mercator (1512–1594), led the way. In the mid-1500s Mercator devised a new projection for his world map that allowed the shape of countries to be shown more accurately. Mercator's projection has been widely used ever since. The geographer ran a flourishing mapmaking business, the success of which was partly founded on new techniques of printing. In 1570 another Flemish cartographer, Abraham Ortelius, produced the first modern atlas, containing 70 maps.

SEE ALSO

♦ Africa
♦ Americas
♦ Exploration
♦ India
♦ Navigation
♦ Portugal
♦ Printing
♦ Spain

Marguerite of Navarre

Marguerite of Navarre (1492–1549) was an important figure in Renaissance France. As sister to the French king Francis I (ruled 1515–1547) she was powerfully placed to support humanists and reformers, and to encourage religious tolerance. She was also a writer of considerable merit. Born in Angoulême in France, the daughter of the count of Angoulême, she was first married to the duke of Alençon but on his death in 1525 married Henry II of Navarre. After the birth of a daughter the couple separated, and Marguerite went to live at her brother's court.

Left: Marguerite of Navarre, painted when she was about 52 by François Clouet (about 1510–1572). As sister to the king of France, Marguerite had considerable influence on French political and religious matters.

Marguerite shared Francis's passion for the arts and literature. She was the patron of a group of writers and thinkers that included her secretary, the Protestant poet Clément Marot (1496–1544). She was deeply pious; and although she remained a Catholic, she supported the work of religious reformers such as Martin Luther and John Calvin, and had some of their works translated into French.

AUTHOR OF PLAYS

Marguerite was also a gifted writer. She wrote plays, which were staged at her brother's court, plus religious poetry. Her most celebrated work, however, is a collection of 72 witty short stories, called the *Heptaméron*, supposedly told by a group of travelers. In her writings Marguerite—like the Protestants—emphasized the importance of an individual's faith and relationship with God. In one of her plays a woman declares: "My heart is my own; my faith is not meant to be given or sold."

Marguerite was also an important political figure. When the emperor Charles V of Spain took Francis I hostage in 1525, she traveled to Madrid to negotiate his release. For a time she was able to use her influence with her brother to stop the persecution of the French Protestants, who were known as Huguenots. In 1534, however, she was powerless to prevent a wave of violence against the Huguenots, who were suspected of wanting to get rid of the monarchy. Even her secretary Marot was forced to flee abroad.

After her brother died in 1547, Marguerite retired from the French court. She did not live long enough to see her grandson, Henry of Navarre, become Henry IV of France in 1589. It was Henry who was finally able to bring an end to the civil war between Catholics and Huguenots.

SEE ALSO
- Calvin
- France
- Francis I
- Luther
- Humanism

Left: A fresco (wall painting) from the early 15th century showing Pope Martin V in 1419 performing the ceremony of consecration for the church of San Egidio in Florence.

Martin V

Pope Martin V (pope 1417–1431) played a vital role in bringing unity to the church after it had been split by what was called the Great Schism. It occurred in 1377, when two rival popes were elected, both claiming to be the head of the church. The dispute was eventually settled at a church council in the city of Constance in southern Germany.

The council lasted from 1414 to 1417 and ended with everyone agreeing to elect Martin as the sole pope. There was a great sense of hope that he would restore the fortunes of the papacy, which had fallen to an all-time low in the previous century.

Born in 1368, Oddone Colonna—the future Martin V—came from a noble Roman family that had, over the years, supplied the church with 27 cardinals. He grew up into a talented, energetic, and determined young man.

A CAREER IN THE CHURCH

Oddone studied at the University of Perugia and became an expert in canon law (the law that deals with church matters). Afterward he held various positions as a diplomat on behalf of the papacy. In 1405 he became a cardinal, and four years later he attended a church council at Pisa that tried—but failed—to resolve the schism. However, it did pave the way for the success of

in 1431 to debate the issue. In the end neither council was able to challenge the supreme position of the pope.

During his years in office Martin proved to be a dynamic leader. He proclaimed a crusade to suppress the followers of the heretic Jan Hus in Bohemia. He tried to get the Greek Orthodox church to accept the authority of the pope in return for help against the Turks, who were threatening its existence. And he abolished certain laws that penalized members of the Jewish faith. Perhaps his most demanding task, however, was the rebuilding of Rome.

THE REBIRTH OF ROME

In the early 14th century the popes had moved away from Rome to take up residence in Avignon in southern France, returning only in 1377. During this time without the papacy, Rome became a second-class city. Great buildings fell into disrepair. The number of citizens dwindled. Plague claimed many lives. There was feuding between the leading families, and the streets were full of violence. Martin now set about restoring the city with his usual vigor. He had churches, bridges, palaces, and other civic buildings rebuilt and declared war on robbers and other criminals. Most of all, the mere fact of his being in residence in Rome at the head of the church brought stability to the city. Merchants also took up residence to do business there, and the city prospered.

Martin had sowed the seeds of the Roman renaissance—within a century it would be one of the finest cities in Europe. He also made vigorous attempts to regain control of the Papal States. After a productive 14-year reign he died in 1431, just before the Council of Basel assembled.

Above: A late 15th-century illustration showing the newly elected Pope Martin V on horseback with the emperor Sigismund walking beside him.

the Council of Constance, when Oddone was elected pope.

After his election Pope Martin V tried to bring much-needed order to the church and to restore the prestige of the papacy. First of all he attempted to resolve the issue of the position of the pope in the church. The Council of Constance had declared that to avoid a repeat of the schism and overcome other problems, a general council, meeting every five years, should become the supreme authority in the church. Martin opposed this idea because he felt that the pope should remain the head of the church. But he did agree to hold a council at Pavia—which soon moved to Siena because of plague—in 1423 and another at Basel

Masaccio

The Italian painter Masaccio (1401–1428) was one of the founding fathers of Renaissance art. He moved away from the popular decorative style known as the International Gothic to create more imposing, lifelike paintings. He was one of the first artists to use the mathematical system called linear perspective to create the illusion of space in his pictures. He also painted light and shadows in a realistic way to draw together the different elements in his work and to give the people and objects he painted a solid appearance.

Masaccio was born in San Giovanni Valdarno, near Florence. His real name was Tommaso di Ser Giovanni di Mone; he was given the nickname "Masaccio," meaning "Sloppy Tom," because of his careless appearance. As a young man, he studied art in Florence. He was influenced by the paintings of Giotto, who had lived nearly a century earlier, as well as by artists of his own time, especially the sculptor Donatello and the architect Filippo Brunelleschi. Through their example he learned to appreciate classical (ancient Greek and Roman) art, and from Brunelleschi he learned the principles of perspective.

EARLY WORK

In 1422, at the age of 21, Masaccio was admitted to the painters' guild in Florence. He was already acknowledged as a master of his art. His earliest surviving work dates from the same year. It is *The Madonna and Child*, the central panel of a triptych (a picture made up of three panels) for a church in Pisa. The Virgin Mary and baby Jesus are portrayed as solid, chunky figures lighted by a single source of light. The work represents a break with the traditional Gothic style of painting, in which artists lighted their subjects with

Above: **The Holy Trinity,** *painted by Masaccio in about 1425. It is the first example of the use of linear perspective in a wall painting.*

Right: Masaccio's painting The Expulsion from Paradise *(1527) in the Brancacci Chapel. Eve's pose, with her arms covering her body, is based on the* Capitoline Venus, *an antique statue popular in the Renaissance.*

the kneeling figures of the people who paid for the painting (the donors), a wealthy merchant and his wife. All are placed in an architectural setting with classical columns that was intended to look like a side chapel opening off the church. Masaccio used perspective to make it look like a real space, and the result amazed his contemporaries.

THE BRANCACCI CHAPEL

Masaccio's masterworks were a series of frescoes painted for the Brancacci Chapel in the church of Santa Maria del Carmine in Florence around 1427. The work was split between Masaccio and the artist Masolino da Panicale. In one large fresco, *The Tribute Money* (see Volume 7, page 55), Masaccio shows Christ flanked by his disciples near a building set in a mountainous landscape. The receding lines of the building, the flowing robes, and the gestures of the disciples all draw the eye to the central, calm figure of Christ. Everything in the picture is unified by sunlight and shadows.

A smaller fresco in the Brancacci Chapel, *The Expulsion from Paradise*, is one of Masaccio's most expressive and revolutionary works. It shows an angel with a sword driving Adam and Eve from the garden of Eden. Adam covers his face in shame, while Eve throws back her head in a despairing wail.

Masaccio died suddenly in 1428 when he was at the height of his powers. However, the grandeur and simplicity of his style influenced generations of artists, all of whom developed his advances in perspective, lighting, and monumental (impressive) figures. In summing up Masaccio's achievements, the 16th-century painter and art historian Giorgio Vasari wrote that he "deserves the same credit as if he had invented art itself."

a flat, even light that cast few shadows. In contrast, the dramatic shadows and lifelike poses of Masaccio's painting were startlingly new.

Masaccio's next major work was probably *The Holy Trinity* (about 1425), a fresco in the church of Santa Maria Novella in Florence. The dignified figure of God the Father stands at the painting's center, holding his son Jesus on the cross. The Holy Spirit in the form of a white dove flutters above the head of Jesus. The trinity is flanked by the Virgin Mary and Saint John the Evangelist, and by

SEE ALSO

♦ Brunelleschi
♦ Classicism
♦ Donatello
♦ Giotto
♦ Gothic Art
♦ Naturalism
♦ Perspective

Mathematics

In the Middle Ages mathematicians tended to study math for its own sake, as a purely intellectual excercise. In the Renaissance, however, mathematicians started to look at how they could put their studies to practical use. This new attitude to mathematical study was helpful in exploring the natural world and paved the way for the scientific revolution of the 1600s.

Two trends fueled this path toward practical math. First, new international trading companies based in Italy needed sophisticated mathematics in order to calculate interest, handle double-entry bookkeeping, and cope with their commercial transactions. Second, the Renaissance witnessed new, clear translations of ancient Greek mathematical works—some new, others replacing older editions made by translators unskilled in mathematics. One notable new edition was Henry Billingsley's English translation (1570) of Euclid's *Elements*, which featured three-dimensional diagrams that popped up out of the book like a child's pop-up book of today. The recovered Greek texts, plus the works of Islamic authors translated in the later Middle Ages, guided Renaissance mathematicians to new achievements.

The mathematics of the Renaissance period tended to fall into one of two camps. On the one hand there was the new class of professional mathematicians that arose in the early 14th century. These men concentrated on practical problems and techniques useful for merchants. On the other hand there were the university professors, who tended toward the more theoretical side. They often kept their best techniques secret, so that they would have an edge when battling other mathematicians in problem-solving competitions—to gain money and fame or simply to keep their jobs.

NEW WAYS WITH NUMBERS

The most important Renaissance innovations came in new ways of writing numbers and mathematical symbols. Medieval Europe had used a wide variety of systems for expressing numbers. The number 1,234, for example, could be written with Roman numerals (MCCXXXIV) or with words ("One thousand two hundred and thirty-four"). The Hindu-Arabic system of our modern numbers had appeared in Europe by the 10th

Below: The Italian mathematician Luca Pacioli (about 1445–1514) with an unknown young man, painted by Jacopo de' Barberi. Pacioli wrote a treatise on accounting in 1494 which contained the first printed explanation of the system of double-entry bookkeeping. He also defined the Golden Section— the ideal ratio used by architects and artists to make their buildings and paintings pleasing and satisfying.

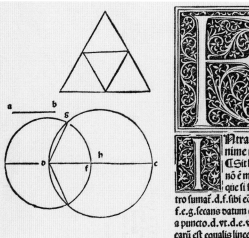

Right: A page from a new edition of Euclid's Elements, *published in Venice in 1482. New translations of ancient mathematical texts were important in helping Renaissance mathematicians build on the achievements of the past.*

century, but it only came into wide-spread use during the Renaissance. Even then some mathematicians continued to use their own variations on these systems (such as writing 1,234 as "1000.200.30.4"). The Hindu-Arabic system made most calculations much easier—an advantage that was especially attractive to merchants.

Several mathematical symbols besides numerals appear prominently in Renaissance texts. Italians frequently used *p* and *m* as plus and minus signs, abbreviating the Italian words *più* ("more") and *meno* ("less"). The modern plus and minus signs ("+" and "−") appeared first in 15th-century Germany, along with a period ("."), which served as an equal sign. In 1557 the Englishman Robert Recorde introduced two parallel lines ("=") to represent the equal sign, "because no two things can be more equal."

THE CUBIC EQUATION

Perhaps the most famous break-through of Renaissance mathematics was the solution of the general cubic equation, which was published in 1545 by the Italian Girolamo Cardano in *Ars Magna* ("The Great Work"). It was an outstanding achievement, since many mathematicians of the time thought the equation was unsolvable.

An example of a cubic equation would be $2x^3 + 4x^2 + 10x + 5 = 0$. Cardano published a formula showing how to find out which values of x would make the sum work. This was a huge step forward in the development of algebra, which is the name given to a type of mathematics in which letters are used to represent unknown numbers. Cardano was also a keen gambler and used his experience with dice and card games to come up with the first theory of probability (the likelihood of a certain event happening, such as rolling a six with a die).

Progress in geometry and trigonometry led to discoveries in mapmaking, astronomy, and the three-dimensional perspective of Renaissance painting. Other applications were less useful: Michael Stifel (1487–1567), one of the greatest German mathematicians of his day, studied "word calculus," a way to interpret a word by associating each of its letters with a number. Using this method on the Bible, Stifel calculated that the world would end on October 18, 1533. When the world survived, he shifted his attention to more reliable algebra.

SEE ALSO

♦ Astronomy
♦ Banking
♦ Merchants
♦ Science
♦ Trade
♦ Universities

Maximilian I

Maximilian I (1459–1519) was Holy Roman emperor in the early part of the 16th century. He was head of the Hapsburg family, and by a series of strategic marriage alliances and military campaigns he added vast territories to the Hapsburgs' traditional lands in Austria. When he died in 1519, the Hapsburgs were the most powerful family in Europe, and his grandson Charles V inherited lands stretching from Spain to Hungary.

Maximilian was born in Wiener Neustadt, Austria, the eldest son of the Holy Roman emperor Frederick III and Leonora of Portugal. As a little boy, he wanted to be a knight and played games of chivalry on his small pony, including mock jousts. Maximilian was just 10 when his father created a new order of chivalry, the knights of Saint George, and the boy was proud to be dedicated as a knight of the order. In later life Maximilian was known as "the last knight"—a symbol of an earlier, chivalrous age.

FIRST MARRIAGE

In 1477 Frederick arranged for the 18-year-old Maximilian to marry Mary of Burgundy. This was an extremely important alliance for the Hapsburgs because it gave them territories in the Low Countries and along the eastern frontier of France, making them a major European power. But first Maximilian had to defend his new lands against attack by King Louis XI of France, and he showed his military ability by defeating the French at the

battle of Guinegate in 1479. When his wife died three years later in a hunting accident, the Netherlandish states rebelled, and Maximilian also defeated them in battle.

In 1486 the Germans elected Maximilian "king of the Romans," the title traditionally given to the emperor's heir. Four years later he married Anne of Brittany by proxy, which means a marriage ceremony was performed in each country without the other partner being present. The marriage would have made a useful alliance against France. Charles VIII of

Above: A portrait of Maximilian (left) and his family, painted by Bernard Strigel about 1515. Maximilian was married twice, and his marriages and other alliances gave him control of vast areas of Europe.

PATRON OF THE ARTS

Maximilian was a great patron of artists and scholars, and was interested in new ideas and in new technology, especially the printing press. He wrote several books himself and planned to write a poetical account of his own life in three volumes. The first, *Theuerdank* ("Precious Thanks"), was a story in 118 verses of his journey to win his first bride, Mary of Burgundy. Each verse was accompanied by an engraving, and Maximilian himself briefed all the artists involved. It was published in 1517, two years before his death; the second and third volumes were only published later. Maximilian also kept many artists busy with ambitious projects, including the German painters Dürer and Altdorfer.

Right: This woodcut of two knights fighting is an illustration from the first edition of Maximilian's story Theuerdank. Maximilian was fascinated by knights and tales of chivalry all his life.

France was unhappy at this prospect, however, and forced Anne to renounce Maximilian and marry him instead.

Maximilian moved to Innsbruck and set about regaining control over his family's traditional lands in Austria, which Hungary had invaded. Then he waged war against Bohemia and secured a treaty by which Bohemian and Hungarian territory would later pass to his family.

EMPEROR AND PATRIARCH

When his father died in 1493, Maximilian succeeded him as emperor. He was now head of the Hapsburg family and ruled over vast territories in Germany, the Low Countries, and Austria. The following year he married Bianca Sforza, daughter of the regent of Milan, and two years later he arranged for his son Philip to marry the Spanish princess Joanna, daughter of Ferdinand and Isabella of Aragon and Castile. Philip died in 1506, but by then all the male heirs of the Spanish monarchs were also dead. The Spanish lands and colonies passed to Joanna and through her to Maximilian's grandsons, Charles and Ferdinand. Maximilian was not always so successful nearer home, however. Many of his plans for reform were blocked by the German princes, and in 1499 he lost in battle to the Swiss Confederation. In the same year he also lost control of possessions in Italy to the French king.

Maximilian died in 1519, age 59, at Wels, on the Danube River, but was buried in Wiener Neustadt, where he had grown up and been made a knight. He had instructed that his heart be taken to Bruges and buried with his beloved Mary of Burgundy, while his elaborate tomb in the cathedral at Innsbruck remained empty.

SEE ALSO

- Charles V
- Dürer
- Germany
- Hapsburg Family
- Holy Roman Empire

Medals and Coins

Medals and coins are similar in appearance and closely related in many ways, but they are used for different purposes. Medals are designed to commemorate a person or event, and coins are used as money. In the Renaissance rulers took a fresh interest in both coins and medals, seeing them as useful ways to spread their reputations and to ensure that their fame lived on in future centuries.

The development of medals and coins in the 15th century reflected the renewed interest in antiquity (ancient Greece and Rome) that characterized the Renaissance. Many antique coins were dug from the ground in the 14th and 15th centuries, when lots of new building work was carried out. They were avidly collected by scholars and rulers, including the writer Petrarch and the powerful Medici family.

Coins were valued not only as precious objects (they were made from gold, silver, and bronze) but also because they provided a direct link with ancient Greek and Roman cultures. The coins had accurate profile portraits (showing the face from the side) and inscriptions identifying the rulers they depicted. From around 300 A.D. these realistic portraits were replaced by more stylized images.

Above: The front of a medal designed by Pisanello in the 1440s featuring a profile portrait of Leonello d'Este, duke of Ferrara. Leonello was an influential figure in the revival of the medal—he had over 10,000 made to various designs.

Renaissance rulers admired the artistic and commemorative value of ancient coins. They realized that portraits on coins and medals provided a good way to spread the fame of the person shown both in their own lifetime and among future generations. The idea of leaving a record of themselves appealed to Renaissance rulers, and in the 1430s they started to commission (order) medals and coins with realistic profile portraits on the front. In so doing, Renaissance leaders also associated themselves with the great rulers and emperors of the classical world.

RENAISSANCE MEDALS

Although medals had been made in ancient times, scholars consider the Renaissance as the most important period in their development. The first Renaissance medal was designed in 1438 by the Italian artist Antonio Pisano, known as Pisanello (about 1393–1455). It commemorates a visit to Italy by the Byzantine emperor John VIII and has a profile portrait of him on the front, while on the reverse he is depicted visiting a shrine. The medal is larger than a coin—it measures about 4 in. (10cm) in diameter—and is made from bronze. Pisanello went on to make medals for many Italian courts in Ferrara, Mantua, Milan, and Naples.

Medals soon became popular in Italy. They were usually made from bronze, although they were also produced in gold and silver. As a rule they were round and larger than coins. Medals made to honor a person had a profile portrait and inscription on the front and an image or symbol relating to that person on the reverse. Medals designed to commemorate events usually had pictures rather than portraits on the front. For example, a medal made in 1506 to mark the start of rebuilding work on Saint Peter's in Rome shows what the planned basilica (church) would look like.

The practice of making medals soon spread from Italy to other European countries, particularly Germany, where Augsburg and Nuremberg were the main centers of production. German medals are sometimes one-sided, with a portrait on the front and a plain reverse. When the reverse is decorated, it is often with a coat of arms, a device that was rarely used in Italy.

Renaissance rulers regarded medals as precious works of art and displayed them alongside their collections of antique coins and gems, often in small, specially designed rooms called *studioli* ("small studies"). They also presented medals as gifts or tokens of thanks. One of the largest collections of medals was owned by Isabella d'Este, marchioness of Mantua. She commissioned a portrait medal of herself that she gave to her favorite writers and had a gold version made for her own collection. It was her favorite portrait of herself, and she displayed it in a diamond-studded frame alongside an antique cameo (a carved gem).

RENAISSANCE COINAGE

By the Renaissance there were already many coins in circulation (use) as a result of flourishing trade. Different countries each had their own coinage, although by the 14th century most produced large gold coins that were based on the florin from the Italian city of Florence. As governments became stronger and more centralized in the 15th century, they were able to exert greater control over the minting (production) of coins. Earlier coins varied greatly because they had been produced by different local rulers, but in the Renaissance their shape and design became more similar.

Large gold coins like florins were the most valuable coins and would have passed through the hands only of wealthy merchants, bankers, and rulers. The same was true of large silver coins, such as thalers, that began to be produced from the 14th century onward. Lower-value coinage made from silver and copper was used by

Below: A gold coin called a ducat made in Milan in the first half of the 15th century. It has a profile portrait of Filippo Maria Visconti, who was duke of Milan from 1412 to 1447.

ordinary people for everyday transactions, such as buying food, and for paying taxes.

From the 1430s powerful Italian families such as the Sforza in Milan, the Este in Ferrara, the Gonzaga in Mantua, and the Montefeltro in Urbino began to issue coins with realistic portraits of themselves on the front. By the end of the 15th century such portraits had become more or less standard on coins made throughout western Europe.

MATERIALS AND TECHNOLOGY
Renaissance developments in coins and medals were fueled by the increased availability of gold and silver from the 15th century onward. Techniques for mining and extracting metal from ore (rock) improved, and substantial new supplies of metal were discovered. New silver mines were opened in Germany and Bohemia, and gold was imported from Africa and, after about 1500, from the Americas.

The technology for making coins and medals also improved. Because medals were often quite large and thick, they were made by pouring molten metal into a mold. Coins, on the other hand, were made by striking the design onto a thin piece of metal. Steel rollers driven by water or horse power were used to roll the metal into thin strips from which coin shapes were then cut. At the beginning of the 16th century a number of different mechanical presses were developed to stamp designs onto the coins, and a similar method was soon used to produce medals.

Coins were weighed before they left the mint because, unlike today, their value was directly related to the amount of precious metal that they contained. In the 16th century measures were introduced to prevent people from trimming the edges off coins when they were in circulation. These "security edges" consisted of inscriptions or milled (serrated) edges.

Above: A print showing how coins were made around the middle of the 15th century.
The man is using a machine to stamp designs onto coins, which then fall into a basket under his workbench.

SEE ALSO

♦ Antiquities
♦ Classicism
♦ Mining
♦ Portraiture
♦ Wealth

Left: The imposing glass-covered courtyard of the Medici villa outside Florence. The paintings on the walls show scenes from the history of the Medici family during the time they ruled Florence in the 15th and 16th centuries.

Medici Family

From the early 15th century to the early 18th century the Medici were the most powerful and influential family in Florence. For most of this time the Medici were rulers of the city, and from the 16th century they also controlled Tuscany, the region of which Florence is the center. They had many enemies who regarded them as tyrants, but on the whole they ruled efficiently and kept Florence out of the wars that were common in Renaissance Italy.

Their influence extended far beyond the city-state of Florence. Four popes and numerous cardinals came from the Medici family, and other members married into European royal families (most notably Catherine de Medici, who became queen of France). In addition to their importance in political and church history the Medici were some of the most magnificent and enlightened art patrons of their time.

BANKERS NOT SOLDIERS

Unlike many ruling families of the time, the Medici did not gain their power through the use of force. They were bankers and merchants rather than soldiers, and their success was based on their wealth and their political astuteness. The origins of the family are obscure, but the name is first recorded in the 12th century. By the

14th century the family had become one of the wealthiest in Florence, but it had various setbacks on its way to power. In 1343 Giovanni de Medici was beheaded after the failure of a plan he had proposed to capture the neighboring city of Lucca, and in 1383 his cousin Salvestro was forced to go into exile after he fell foul of rivals.

HEAD OF THE COUNCIL

The real founder of the family's success was Giovanni de Bicci de Medici (1360–1429), whose father was a textile merchant and ran a banking business. Giovanni became one of the wealthiest bankers in Italy before turning to politics. His political career culminated in 1421, when he became *gonfalonier* (head of the council that governed Florence). He also began the Medici tradition of patronizing the best artists and architects of the time. Most notably, he helped finance one of Filippo Brunelleschi's masterpieces, the church of San Lorenzo.

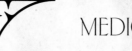

MEDICI POPES

Four members of the Medici dynasty became pope: Leo X (pope 1513–1521), Clement VII (pope 1523–1534), Pius IV (pope 1559–1565), and Leo XI, who died within a month of taking office in 1605. The most famous was Leo X, who was born Giovanni de Medici in 1475, the second son of Lorenzo the Magnificent. He was one of the most extravagant of Renaissance popes, spending huge amounts on his own pleasures as well as on wars and artistic projects, particularly the rebuilding of Saint Peter's in Rome, which had been initiated by his predecessor Julius II. His recklessness left the papal treasury deeply in debt.

Giovanni's eldest son, Cosimo (1389–1464), inherited a vast fortune from his father. After a tempestuous start to his political career, which included a spell in prison and a death sentence commuted to banishment, he became in 1434 effectively the ruler of Florence, although in theory he was just an ordinary citizen like the rest of the population. Because Florence

Left: A 16th-century tapestry in wool and silk showing Cosimo the Elder with his architects and advisers examining a model of a building he was planning to erect in Florence.

Above: A portrait of Lorenzo the Magnificent, painted by Giorgio Vasari (1511–1574). Poet, scholar, and patron of the arts, Lorenzo presided over a golden age in Florence's history.

the Medici Palace (begun 1445), designed by Michelozzo. It is large and imposing, but also austere, and it is said that Cosimo rejected a design by his friend Brunelleschi because it was too elaborate and would inspire envy. Cosimo also commissioned work from many artists, including the painters Uccello and Fra Angelico and the sculptors Ghiberti and Donatello. He was also a major collector of

---

Cosimo set Florence on the road to becoming the flower of Renaissance Italy

---

manuscripts and founded the Medici Library, which (now renamed the Laurentian Library) has one of the most important collections of manuscripts and rare books in Italy.

Cosimo was succeeded by his son Piero (1416–1469), known as Piero the Gouty. Despite being severely crippled by gout, Piero managed to defeat a conspiracy against him and remained ruler of Florence for five years until his death in 1469. He is probably best remembered for commissioning one of the most beautiful frescoes (wall paintings) of the 15th century—*The Journey of the Magi* (1459–1461) by Benozzo Gozzoli in the chapel of the Medici Palace. The fresco depicts a glittering cavalcade of figures as the Magi (wise men) travel to see the new-born Jesus. One of the figures is said to be a portrait of Piero.

Piero's son and successor was the most famous member of the family, Lorenzo de Medici (1449–1492), known as Lorenzo the Magnificent, whose period of rule is regarded as one

prided itself on being a republic, governed by the people rather than by hereditary rulers, Cosimo was never ostentatious in his use of power. He preferred to bankrupt his enemies through clever financial maneuverings rather than murder them, as many Renaissance rulers would have.

A GREAT PATRON OF THE ARTS

Cosimo was one of the great Medici patrons of the arts, and he set Florence on the road to becoming the flower of Renaissance Italy. He commissioned many buildings by the architects Brunelleschi and Michelozzo di Bartolommeo, but his pet project was of the most glorious ages in Florence's history. Lorenzo was highly cultured and a skillful politician, but he was not a good businessman, and he greatly reduced the family wealth through his lavish spending on the arts and spectacular entertainments such as carnivals, balls, and tournaments.

CONSPIRACY TO KILL

In 1478 there was a plot against Lorenzo's life by the rival Pazzi family of bankers. The assassins killed Lorenzo's brother, Giuliano, but Lorenzo managed to escape with only slight injuries. The conspirators were seized by the Florentine crowd and torn to pieces. His survival of the conspiracy increased Lorenzo's popularity and strengthened his power. Although in theory he was just a private citizen in a constitutional republic, he was more like the king of Florence.

Lorenzo was a poet and scholar and was friendly with many of the leading literary figures of the day. He had magnificent collections of Roman antiquities, including sculptures, vases, and gems, and he also encouraged and nurtured many artists, including Botticelli, Verrocchio, Leonardo da Vinci, and the young Michelangelo, who for a time lived in the Medici Palace and was treated by Lorenzo almost as an adopted son.

Lorenzo was succeeded by his son Piero (1471–1503), known as Piero the Unfortunate. In 1494 Piero made humiliating concessions to Charles VIII of France, who had invaded Italy, and that lost him the confidence of the people of Florence, who forced him into exile. For the next 18 years the Medici stayed away from Florence, but in 1512 another of Lorenzo's sons, Giuliano (1479–1516), returned and assumed power. The family remained

QUEEN OF FRANCE

Catherine de Medici (1519–1589) was the great-granddaughter of Lorenzo the Magnificent. Orphaned within a few days of her birth, she was raised and educated by nuns. When she was 14, her uncle, Pope Clement VII, arranged for her to marry the duke of Orleans, who in 1547 became King Henry II of France, making Catherine queen of France.

Catherine bore Henry 10 children, of whom seven survived infancy. Three of her sons became king in turn after Henry's death in 1559: Francis II (ruled 1559–1560), Charles IX (ruled 1560–1574), and Henry III (ruled 1574–1589). Catherine acted as regent or adviser to all three and played an important role in French history at a time when the country was torn by civil war between Catholics and Protestants. Despite Catherine's attempts throughout this troubled time to achieve peace and religious tolerance, she was blamed for the Saint Bartholomew's Day Massacre (1572) in Paris, in which thousands of Protestants were killed in mob violence. Catherine died in 1589, eight months before the murder of her third son Henry III and the accession of Henry of Navarre, who as King Henry IV brought peace to France by granting Protestants equal rights with Catholics.

A 16th-century portrait of Catherine de Medici, queen of France. Three of her sons became king of France in turn.

Right: A corridor in the Uffizi Gallery, built by Cosimo de Medici the Younger. Cosimo asked Giorgio Vasari to design a large building that would house all the administrative offices of Florence under one roof. The result was a palatial building that was simply called the Uffizi ("Offices"). It is now a famous art gallery.

in control until 1527, when it was again expelled following another political crisis. This time it was only three years before the Medici returned, and in 1532 Alessandro (1511–1537), the illegitimate son of Giulio de Medici (Pope Clement VII), assumed the title of duke of Florence.

COSIMO THE YOUNGER

Alessandro ruled the city by terror, and in 1537 he was assassinated. He was succeeded by a distant cousin, Cosimo de Medici the Younger (1519–1574), who was backed by a group of influential citizens and by the Holy Roman emperor Charles V. Cosimo was only 17 when he came to power, but he soon stamped his authority on Florence. He was a strong and clever ruler who gave the city a degree of stability it had not enjoyed for many years. In 1557, by a combination of brains and brawn, he gained possession of the rival city of Siena and most of its dependent territories. That gave him control of a large area of Tuscany, and in 1569 he assumed the title of grand duke of Tuscany, a title that he was able to pass on to his descendants.

Unlike many members of his family, Cosimo was not a real connoisseur of art, but he realized its value as propaganda, and he spent a great deal of money on glorifying both himself and Florence. He redecorated the interior of the Palazzo Vecchio and designed the great Boboli Gardens of Florence. His favorite painter was Agnolo Bronzino, and among the other artists he employed were Benvenuto Cellini, Giambologna, and Giorgio Vasari. To streamline public services, Cosimo had Vasari design a single building to house them all. It was called the Uffizi ("Offices"), and it is now one of the most famous art galleries in the world.

Cosimo was perhaps the last of the great Medici rulers, but the dynasty continued until 1737, when Grand Duke Gian Gastone de Medici died without a male heir, and the title passed to a distant relative, Francis Stephen, duke of Lorraine.

Medicine and Surgery

At the beginning of the 15th century the practice of medicine in Europe was still dominated by the ideas of the Greek physician Galen, who lived in the second century A.D., as it had been throughout the Middle Ages. However, during the Renaissance period many new ideas began to appear that were destined to transform medical practice and would lay the foundations of today's medicine.

Above: A 15th-century wall painting showing physicians and monks treating the sick in a hospital in Siena. Most hospitals of the Renaissance were run by monasteries or other religious foundations.

position of the planets in the sky affected a person's health, so that when the signs were favorable, the patient might recover.

There were many different kinds of people practicing medicine. The most highly skilled were the physicians. They were trained at the medical schools of the universities and learned to diagnose and treat disease, and sometimes to carry out surgery. They charged high fees. Next down the scale were surgeons, many of whom were barber-surgeons. There were also midwives, who learned by experience how to help women in childbirth, and apothecaries, who learned about herbal remedies through apprenticeship and experience. At the bottom of the scale were noblewomen, who looked after the health of their family and servants with simple herbal remedies, and monks, who ran infirmaries attached to monasteries and treated the sick in the local community.

The ancient Greek physician Galen believed that the human body contained four kinds of fluid—blood, yellow bile, black bile, and phlegm—which he called "humors." A person became sick, he said, when the humors were out of balance. So the way to restore a person to health was to restore the balance. That was usually done by bleeding, which involved making a cut in the arm of the patient and allowing a large quantity of blood to flow out.

COMMON TREATMENTS

This practice remained one of the major medical treatments for disease throughout the Renaissance. Doctors also prescribed herbal remedies, special diets, rest, and fasting (advising the patient to stop eating until better). Physicians also believed that the

The new spirit of inquiry that characterized the Renaissance led doctors to start questioning the validity of Galen's theory of humors. Medical knowledge in Islam was more advanced than in Europe, and Arabian physicians were skilled in the use of chemically prepared medicines. An important

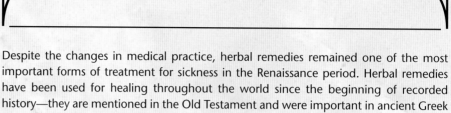

HERBAL MEDICINE

Below: An illustration showing a doctor bleeding a patient, from a 15th-century manuscript on the plague. Bloodletting was a common treatment in Renaissance times—it was believed it would help the patient recover by restoring the balance of the humors.

Despite the changes in medical practice, herbal remedies remained one of the most important forms of treatment for sickness in the Renaissance period. Herbal remedies have been used for healing throughout the world since the beginning of recorded history—they are mentioned in the Old Testament and were important in ancient Greek and Roman times. Several ancient Greeks wrote about the medicinal properties of herbs, including Hippocrates, Discorides, and Galen. In India, Arabia, China, and the early societies of Africa and the Americas the special properties of plants have always been harnessed to cure sickness.

Herbal remedies were prepared by apothecaries, who also advised on their use. For example, sage might be prescribed as a treatment for the palsy, while syrup of violets was recommended as a cure for epilepsy, pleurisy, jaundice, quinsy, and many other ailments. Some herbal treatments relied on the doctrine of signatures, which said that a plant carried on it signs of its use in healing. The kernel of a walnut, for example, with its wrinkled skin resembled a brain and so could be used to treat mental diseases.

medical textbook at the time was the *Canon of Medicine* by the Persian physician Avicenna (980–1037). It was based on the medical knowledge of both the ancient Greeks and Islam, and it encouraged physicians to rely more on experience than on ancient dogma.

PARACELSUS THE RADICAL

One European doctor in tune with this idea was Paracelsus (about 1493–1542), a Swiss physician who challenged the basic ideas of Galenic medicine. He suggested that disease was caused by external factors rather than by an internal imbalance of the humors. He also argued that physicians should use their senses and experience to learn about disease.

Paracelsus's most important contribution to European medical science, however, was his use of chemical remedies. He developed a range of chemical drugs based on mercury, iron, copper sulfate, and sulfur to treat many serious diseases. Meanwhile, travelers to the East and the New World were also bringing back new drugs to

Europe. Sassafras from the West Indies was used in Spain to treat the plague, while guaiac wood, also from the Americas, was used as a cure for syphilis and other diseases.

Anatomical knowledge also advanced during the Renaissance. The ban on dissecting human bodies was lifted in several medical schools, and physicians were able to make their own observations about how the body was constructed. In 1543 Andreas Vesalius (1514–1564), physician to the emperor Charles V, published a revolutionary book on anatomy entitled *De Humani Corporis Fabrica* ("On the Structure of the Human Body"). The book was illustrated with detailed anatomical drawings based on many dissections Vesalius had carried out on the corpses of executed criminals. It was the most accurate anatomical reference work published to date, correcting over 200 errors in Galen's anatomy.

BRUTAL SURGERY

Surgery was a more practical craft than medicine, less concerned with treating disease and more with setting broken bones and amputating limbs. Many surgeons during the Middle Ages had been untrained barber-surgeons, but during the Renaissance moves were made to regulate the training of surgeons. Guilds of barber-surgeons were formed, which supervised apprenticeships and examinations, and some Spanish and Italian universities also taught surgery. Surgeons dealt with dentistry (extracting bad teeth), burns, wounds, broken bones, and amputations. Most operations were carried out without painkillers, although some lucky patients might have their senses dulled with opium or alcohol. Many patients died soon after surgery, either from infection or shock.

Some significant advances in surgery were made in the 16th century. Rhinoplasty—nose reconstruction—became important in an age when syphilis often damaged the nasal cartilage. The French army surgeon Ambroise Paré (1510–1590) began treating gunshot wounds in a revolutionary way. Instead of cauterizing them with a hot iron or boiling oil, which was supposed to negate the poison of gunpowder, he tied off the arteries, treated the wound with salves, and bound it with bandages. Paré also developed more sophisticated artificial limbs than those used before.

Above: A surgeon amputating a leg, an illustration from a 16th-century medical textbook.

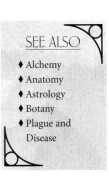

SEE ALSO

♦ Alchemy
♦ Anatomy
♦ Astrology
♦ Botany
♦ Plague and Disease

Merchants

Above: Hans Holbein's portrait of the German merchant George Gisze. Gisze operated out of the Steelyard, an area of London that was home to a cooperative of German merchants.

Merchants in the Renaissance played an important role in society. They satisfied a growing population's demands for material goods, and in doing so they also dealt in money—making loans, speculating on fluctuations in rates of exchange, and financing other people's ventures. The merchants' financial transactions brought them into contact with the most influential people in Europe, and their decisions could make or break an individual—even someone as powerful as a king. In addition, their great wealth enabled them to become patrons of the arts.

During the 15th and 16th centuries there was a great increase in the population of Europe. This population increase stimulated the trade in basic necessities, such as foodstuffs, textiles, and timber. From the richer elements of society there was also demand for luxury goods such as glass, ceramics, silverware, fine Persian rugs, and tapestries. Even the frequent conflicts that occurred in the 15th and 16th centuries brought their own demands. Metals such as iron, copper, and tin were needed for armor and weapons, while sulfur and wood were required for manufacturing gunpowder. The trade in these products allowed merchants to become extremely wealthy.

LONG-DISTANCE TRADE

The majority of trade in the Renaissance period took place on a local level as farmers and craftsmen sold their wares to people who lived nearby. However, the period saw a substantial growth in long-distance trade overseen by merchants who operated on a highly sophisticated level.

For example, although much food such as eggs and dairy products was bought and sold locally, the trade in other foodstuffs could be carried out on a much larger scale. There was a huge amount of money to be made from dealing in grain. Grain was often transported all the way across Europe to take advantage of local shortages, even though the journey could take many months. Grain merchants stood to make huge profits from their activities and were often the target of public resentment.

During the medieval period most merchants traveled to oversee the transportation of their goods, which could go through many sets of hands on their long journeys. By the 15th century, however, richer merchants tended to remain in their home towns. They sent out agents to foreign countries, where they conducted local business, became proficient in local trading customs, and arranged for the goods to be shipped back to the company's warehouses. Merchants needed to be able to trust their agents totally, so they usually sent members of their own family.

RISKS OF TRADE

Although long-distance trade could be extremely profitable, it also carried huge risks since cargoes could be lost at sea or stolen. Merchants reduced the risks by forming partnerships in which both the profits and losses were shared with a number of investors. Merchants also tried to deal in as many different types of product as possible in case the price of one type of good fell sharply. They also took out insurance, which had developed slowly from the 14th century onward.

Trade was also made safer by the use of bills of exchange. The bill was a letter in which the seller of goods in one place instructed the buyer of goods to pay a certain sum of money to a third person in another place. So a London merchant who bought goods in Venice might pay the Venetian agent in London. No funds actually traveled across Europe, making the whole transaction safe and secure.

Below: This 15th-century manuscript illustration shows merchants buying and selling cloth at a market in Bologna in Italy. The textile trade was extremely important in the Renaissance period.

TRADE FAIRS

The great trade fairs of medieval Europe continued to flourish in the Renaissance. These seasonal gatherings took place at a number of cities that were strategically located along major trade routes. Merchants and their agents came from all over Europe to acquire a vast selection of goods.

The most important regional fairs of the Renaissance were at Medina del Campo in Spain, Prato in Italy, Lublin in Poland, and Leipzig in Germany. The most important international gatherings were at Lyon in France and Frankfurt-am-Main in Germany. A list of the items purchased by one Lübeck-based merchant at the Frankfurt trade fair in 1495 gives some indication of the range of goods available. It mentions spices, coats of mail, weapons, velvet, silver goblets and plates, gold rings and chains, pearls, brooches, and northern Italian paper.

Often the date that the money was to be paid to the seller was set some time in the future. This practice allowed richer merchants to enter the world of banking by providing loans and charging interest. Among the most famous families of merchant bankers were the Medici and Datini of Florence, Italy, and the Fuggers of Augsburg, Germany. The rich banking families maintained an overview of international affairs and commercial trends. They wielded considerable political influence in their cities and among the royal families of Europe, who depended on them to raise the money for major ventures, such as dynastic marriages or warfare. For example, the Fugger family of Germany financed Charles V's campaign to become Holy Roman emperor.

THE FUGGERS

The Fuggers are a good example of a family that began simply as merchants but used their wealth to expand into other areas. The founder of the dynasty, Hans Fugger (1348–1409), was a weaver who built up a successful textile trade in Augsburg in the late 14th century. His son Jakob expanded the firm's international trade, but it was Hans' grandson, Jakob II, "the Rich" (1459–1525), who transformed the fortunes of the Fugger dynasty. By

Right: A 15th-century Italian painting of a merchant taking sacks of wool by donkey to Siena in Italy. While poorer merchants traveled with their goods, their richer counterparts stayed in their home towns and employed agents to travel in their place.

Left: A print from the late 16th century showing merchants unloading their goods in Lisbon harbor. In the 16th century Portuguese traders grew rich importing spices from east Asia.

granting permanent loans to the copper- and silver-mining enterprises in the Austrian Alps, he became a partner in a hugely profitable business.

Jakob then moved into all areas of international commerce, including the spice trade, and invested heavily in land, property, textiles, and precious stones. The Fuggers also expanded their mining interests, investing in Hungarian copper mines as well.

This move was particularly shrewd. Copper was used not only in armaments manufacture but also to pay for spices. The metal was in high demand in Egypt and India, and was therefore as acceptable as silver as payment. By the beginning of the 16th century the Fuggers had established a virtual monopoly in copper. Between 1526 and 1529 the family exported almost 3,300 tons (3,000 tonnes) of the metal, which earned them a profit of over a million ducats.

The wealth and power of the most influential merchants led to them being viewed with mistrust by the nobility, who often looked down on them because of their lowly birth. One way in which rich merchants attempted to raise their social status was by becoming patrons of the arts. For example, the 15th-century Florentine merchant Giovanni Rucellai commissioned works by the scholar and architect Leon Battista Alberti and the painter Paolo Uccello.

Often the works of art that were commissioned were simply portraits of the merchants themselves. Among the most famous was Hans Holbein's 16th-century painting of George Gisze, a merchant from Danzig in Germany who was based in London (see page 64). Holbein's portrait shows Gisze surrounded by the tools of the merchant's trade, including a set of scales, a seal, and writing implements.

SEE ALSO

♦ Bankers and Banking
♦ Capitalism
♦ Holbein
♦ Manufacturing
♦ Medici Family
♦ Mining
♦ Population
♦ Textiles
♦ Trade
♦ Wealth

Timeline

♦ **1305** Giotto begins work on frescoes for the Arena Chapel, Padua—he is often considered the father of Renaissance art.

♦ **1321** Dante publishes the *Divine Comedy*, which has a great influence on later writers.

♦ **1327** Petrarch begins writing the sonnets known as the *Canzoniere*.

♦ **1337** The start of the Hundred Years' War between England and France.

♦ **1353** Boccaccio writes the *Decameron*, an influential collection of 100 short stories.

♦ **1368** The Ming dynasty comes to power in China.

♦ **1377** Pope Gregory XI moves the papacy back to Rome from Avignon, where it has been based since 1309.

♦ **1378** The Great Schism begins: two popes, Urban VI and Clement VII, both lay claim to the papacy.

♦ **1378** English theologian John Wycliffe criticizes the practices of the Roman Catholic church.

♦ **1380** Ivan I of Muscovy defeats the army of the Mongol Golden Horde at the battle of Kulikovo.

♦ **1389** The Ottomans defeat the Serbs at the battle of Kosovo, beginning a new phase of Ottoman expansion.

♦ **1397** Sigismund of Hungary is defeated by the Ottoman Turks at the battle of Nicopolis.

♦ **1397** Queen Margaret of Denmark unites Denmark, Sweden, and Norway under the Union of Kalmar.

♦ **1398** The Mongol leader Tamerlane invades India.

♦ **1399** Henry Bolingbroke becomes Henry IV of England.

♦ **1400** English writer Geoffrey Chaucer dies, leaving his *Canterbury Tales* unfinished.

♦ **1403** In Italy the sculptor Ghiberti wins a competition to design a new set of bronze doors for Florence Cathedral.

♦ **c.1402** The Bohemian preacher Jan Hus begins to attack the corruption of the church.

♦ **1405** The Chinese admiral Cheng Ho commands the first of seven expeditions to the Indian Ocean and East Africa.

♦ **1415** Jan Hus is summoned to the Council of Constance and condemned to death.

♦ **1415** Henry V leads the English to victory against the French at the battle of Agincourt.

♦ **c.1415** Florentine sculptor Donatello produces his sculpture *Saint George*.

♦ **1416** Venice defeats the Ottoman fleet at the battle of Gallipoli, but does not check the Ottoman advance.

♦ **1417** The Council of Constance elects Martin V pope, ending the Great Schism.

♦ **1418** Brunelleschi designs the dome of Florence Cathedral.

♦ **1420** Pope Martin V returns the papacy to Rome, bringing peace and order to the city.

♦ **c.1420** Prince Henry of Portugal founds a school of navigation at Sagres, beginning a great age of Portuguese exploration.

♦ **1422** Charles VI of France dies, leaving his throne to the English king Henry VI. Charles VI's son also claims the throne.

♦ **c.1425** Florentine artist Masaccio paints the *Holy Trinity*, the first painting to use the new science of perspective.

♦ **1429** Joan of Arc leads the French to victory at Orléans; Charles VII is crowned king of France in Reims Cathedral.

♦ **1431** The English burn Joan of Arc at the stake for heresy.

♦ **1433** Sigismund of Luxembourg becomes Holy Roman emperor.

♦ **1434** Cosimo de Medici comes to power in Florence.

♦ **1434** The Flemish artist Jan van Eyck paints the *Arnolfini Marriage* using the newly developed medium of oil paint.

♦ **1439** The Council of Florence proclaims the reunion of the Western and Orthodox churches.

♦ **c.1440** Donatello completes his statue of David—the first life-size bronze sculpture since antiquity.

♦ **1443** Federigo da Montefeltro becomes ruler of Urbino.

♦ **1447** The Milanese people declare their city a republic.

♦ **1450** The condottiere Francesco Sforza seizes control of Milan.

♦ **1450** Fra Angelico paints *The Annunciation* for the monastery of San Marco in Florence.

♦ **1453** Constantinople, capital of the Byzantine Empire, falls to the Ottomans and becomes the capital of the Muslim Empire.

♦ **1453** The French defeat the English at the battle of Castillon, ending the Hundred Years' War.

♦ **1454–1456** Venice, Milan, Florence, Naples, and the papacy form the Italian League to maintain peace in Italy.

♦ **1455** The start of the Wars of the Roses between the Houses of York and Lancaster in England.

♦ **c.1455** The German Johannes Gutenberg develops the first printing press using movable type.

♦ **1456** The Florentine painter Uccello begins work on the *Battle of San Romano*.

♦ **1461** The House of York wins the Wars of the Roses; Edward IV becomes king of England.

♦ **1461** Sonni Ali becomes king of the Songhai Empire in Africa.

♦ **1462** Marsilio Ficino founds the Platonic Academy of Florence— the birthplace of Renaissance Neoplatonism.

♦ **1463** War breaks out between Venice and the Ottoman Empire.

♦ **1465** The Italian painter Mantegna begins work on the Camera degli Sposi in Mantua.

♦ **1467** Civil war breaks out in Japan, lasting for over a century.

♦ **1469** Lorenzo the Magnificent, grandson of Cosimo de Medici, comes to power in Florence.

♦ **1469** The marriage of Isabella I of Castile and Ferdinand V of Aragon unites the two kingdoms.

♦ **1470** The Florentine sculptor Verrocchio completes his *David*.

♦ **1476** William Caxton establishes the first English printing press at Westminster, near London.

♦ **1477** Pope Sixtus IV begins building the Sistine Chapel.

♦ **c.1477** Florentine painter Sandro Botticelli paints the *Primavera*, one of the first large-scale mythological paintings of the Renaissance.

♦ **1478** The Spanish Inquisition is founded in Spain.

♦ **1480** The Ottoman fleet destroys the port of Otranto in south Italy.

♦ **1485** Henry Tudor becomes Henry VII of England—the start of the Tudor dynasty.

♦ **1486** *The Witches' Hammer* is published, a handbook on how to hunt down witches.

♦ **1488** Portuguese navigator Bartholomeu Dias reaches the Cape of Good Hope.

♦ **1491** Missionaries convert King Nzina Nkowu of the Congo to Christianity.

♦ **1492** The Spanish monarchs conquer Granada, the last Moorish territory in Spain.

♦ **1492** Christopher Columbus lands in the Bahamas, claiming the territory for Spain.

♦ **1492** Henry VII of England renounces all English claims to the French throne.

♦ **1493** The Hapsburg Maximilian becomes Holy Roman emperor.

♦ **1494** Charles VIII of France invades Italy, beginning four decades of Italian wars.

♦ **1494** In Italy Savonarola comes to power in Florence.

♦ **1494** The Treaty of Tordesillas divides the non-Christian world between Spain and Portugal.

♦ **1495** Leonardo da Vinci begins work on *The Last Supper* .

♦ **1495** Spain forms a Holy League with the Holy Roman emperor and expels the French from Naples.

♦ **1498** Portuguese navigator Vasco da Gama reaches Calicut, India.

♦ **1498** German artist Dürer creates the *Apocalypse* woodcuts.

♦ **1500** Portuguese navigator Pedro Cabral discovers Brazil.

♦ **c.1500–1510** Dutch painter Hieronymus Bosch paints *The Garden of Earthly Delights*.

♦ **c.1502** Italian architect Donato Bramante designs the Tempietto Church in Rome.

♦ **1503** Leonardo da Vinci begins painting the *Mona Lisa*.

♦ **1504** Michelangelo finishes his statue of David, widely seen as a symbol of Florence.

♦ **c.1505** Venetian artist Giorgione paints *The Tempest*.

♦ **1506** The Italian architect Donato Bramante begins work on rebuilding Saint Peter's, Rome.

♦ **1508** Michelangelo begins work on the ceiling of the Sistine Chapel in the Vatican.

♦ **1509** Henry VIII ascends the throne of England.

♦ **1509** The League of Cambrai defeats Venice at the battle of Agnadello.

♦ **1510–1511** Raphael paints *The School of Athens* in the Vatican.

♦ **1511** The French are defeated at the battle of Ravenna in Italy and are forced to retreat over the Alps.

♦ **1513** Giovanni de Medici becomes Pope Leo X.

♦ **1515** Thomas Wolsey becomes lord chancellor of England.

♦ **1515** Francis I becomes king of France. He invades Italy and captures Milan.

♦ **c.1515** German artist Grünewald paints the *Isenheim Altarpiece*.

♦ **1516** Charles, grandson of the emperor Maximilian I, inherits the Spanish throne as Charles I.

♦ **1516** Thomas More publishes his political satire *Utopia*.

♦ **1516** Dutch humanist Erasmus publishes a more accurate version of the Greek New Testament.

♦ **1517** Martin Luther pins his 95 theses on the door of the castle church in Wittenburg.

♦ **1519** Charles I of Spain becomes Holy Roman emperor Charles V.

♦ **1519–1521** Hernán Cortés conquers Mexico for Spain.

♦ **1520** Henry VIII of England and Francis I of France meet at the Field of the Cloth of Gold to sign a treaty of friendship.

♦ **1520** Portuguese navigator Ferdinand Magellan discovers a route to the Indies around the tip of South America.

♦ **1520** Süleyman the Magnificent becomes ruler of the Ottoman Empire, which now dominates the eastern Mediterranean.

♦ **1520–1523** Titian paints *Bacchus and Ariadne* for Alfonso d'Este.

♦ **1521** Pope Leo X excommuicates Martin Luther.

♦ **1521** The emperor Charles V attacks France, beginning a long period of European war.

♦ **1522** Ferdinand Magellan's ship the *Victoria* is the first to sail around the world.

♦ **1523–1525** Huldrych Zwingli sets up a Protestant church at Zurich in Switzerland.

♦ **1525** In Germany the Peasants' Revolt is crushed, and its leader, Thomas Münzer, is executed.

♦ **1525** The emperor Charles V defeats the French at the battle of Pavia and takes Francis I prisoner.

♦ **1525** William Tyndale translates the New Testament into English.

♦ **1526** The Ottoman Süleyman the Magnificent defeats Hungary at the battle of Mohács.

♦ **1526** Muslim Mongol leader Babur invades northern India and establishes the Mogul Empire.

♦ **c.1526** The Italian artist Correggio paints the *Assumption of the Virgin* in Parma Cathedral.

♦ **1527** Charles V's armies overrun Italy and sack Rome.

♦ **1527–1530** Gustavus I founds a Lutheran state church in Sweden.

♦ **1528** Italian poet and humanist Baldassare Castiglione publishes *The Courtier*.

♦ **1529** The Ottoman Süleyman the Magnificent lays siege to Vienna, but eventually retreats.

♦ **1530** The Catholic church issues the "Confutation," attacking Luther and Protestantism.

♦ **1531** The Protestant princes of Germany form the Schmalkaldic League.

♦ **1531–1532** Francisco Pizarro conquers Peru for Spain.

♦ **1532** Machiavelli's *The Prince* is published after his death.

♦ **1533** Henry VIII of England rejects the authority of the pope and marries Anne Boleyn.

♦ **1533** Anabaptists take over the city of Münster in Germany.

♦ **1533** Christian III of Denmark founds the Lutheran church of Denmark.

♦ **1534** Paul III becomes pope and encourages the growth of new religious orders such as the Jesuits.

♦ **1534** Luther publishes his German translation of the Bible.

♦ **1534** The Act of Supremacy declares Henry VIII supreme head of the Church of England.

♦ **c.1535** Parmigianino paints the mannerist masterpiece *Madonna of the Long Neck*.

♦ **1535–1536** The Swiss city of Geneva becomes Protestant and expels the Catholic clergy.

♦ **1536** Calvin publishes *Institutes of the Christian Religion*, which sets out his idea of predestination.

♦ **1536** Pope Paul III sets up a reform commission to examine the state of the Catholic church.

♦ **1537** Hans Holbein is appointed court painter to Henry VIII of England.

♦ **1539** Italian painter Bronzino begins working for Cosimo de Medici the Younger in Florence.

♦ **1539** Ignatius de Loyola founds the Society of Jesus (the Jesuits).

♦ **1541** John Calvin sets up a model Christian city in Geneva.

♦ **1543** Andreas Vesalius publishes *On the Structure of the Human Body*, a handbook of anatomy based on dissections.

♦ **1543** Polish astronomer Copernicus's *On the Revolutions of the Heavenly Spheres* proposes a sun-centered universe.

♦ **1544** Charles V and Francis I of France sign the Truce of Crespy.

♦ **1545** Pope Paul III organizes the Council of Trent to counter the threat of Protestantism.

♦ **1545** Spanish explorers find huge deposits of silver in the Andes Mountains of Peru.

♦ **1547** Charles V defeats the Protestant Schmalkaldic League at the Battle of Mühlberg.

♦ **1547** Ivan IV "the Terrible" declares himself czar of Russia.

♦ **1548** Titian paints the equestrian portrait *Charles V after the Battle of Mühlberg*.

♦ **1548** Tintoretto paints *Saint Mark Rescuing the Slave*.

♦ **1550** Italian Georgio Vasari publishes his *Lives of the Artists*.

♦ **1553** Mary I of England restores the Catholic church.

♦ **1554** Work begins on the Cathedral of Saint Basil in Red Square, Moscow.

♦ **1555** At the Peace of Augsburg Charles V allows the German princes to determine their subjects' religion.

♦ **1556** Ivan IV defeats the last Mongol khanates. Muscovy now dominates the Volga region.

♦ **1556** Philip II becomes king of Spain.

♦ **1559** Elizabeth I of England restores the Protestant church.

♦ **1562** The Wars of Religion break out in France.

♦ **1565** Flemish artist Pieter Bruegel the Elder paints *Hunters in the Snow*.

♦ **1565** Italian architect Palladio designs the Villa Rotunda, near Vicenza.

♦ **1566** The Dutch revolt against the Spanish over the loss of political and religious freedoms:

Philip II of Spain sends 10,000 troops under the duke of Alba to suppress the revolt.

♦ **1569** Flemish cartographer Mercator produces a world map using a new projection.

♦ **1571** Philip II of Spain and an allied European force defeat the Ottomans at the battle of Lepanto.

♦ **1572** In Paris, France, a Catholic mob murders thousands of Huguenots in the Saint Bartholomew's Day Massacre.

♦ **1572** Danish astronomer Tycho Brahe sees a new star.

♦ **1573** Venetian artist Veronese paints the *Feast of the House of Levi*.

♦ **1579** The seven northern provinces of the Netherlands form the Union of Utrecht.

♦ **1580** Giambologna creates his mannerist masterpiece *Flying Mercury*.

♦ **1585** Henry III of France bans Protestantism in France; civil war breaks out again in the War of the Three Henrys.

♦ **1586** El Greco, a Greek artist active in Spain, paints the *Burial of Count Orgaz*.

♦ **1587** Mary, Queen of Scots, is executed by Elizabeth I of England.

♦ **c.1587** Nicholas Hilliard paints the miniature *Young Man among Roses*.

♦ **1588** Philip II of Spain launches his great Armada against England —but the fleet is destroyed.

♦ **1589** Henry of Navarre becomes king of France as Henry IV.

♦ **1592–1594** Tintoretto paints *The Last Supper*.

♦ **1596** Edmund Spencer publishes the *Faerie Queene*, glorifying Elizabeth I as "Gloriana."

♦ **1598** Henry IV of France grants Huguenots and Catholics equal political rights.

♦ **1598** In England the Globe Theater is built on London's south bank; it stages many of Shakespeare's plays.

♦ **1600–1601** Caravaggio paints *The Crucifixion of Saint Peter*, an early masterpiece of baroque art.

♦ **1603** Elizabeth I of England dies and is succeeded by James I, son of Mary, Queen of Scots.

♦ **1610** Galileo's *The Starry Messenger* supports the sun-centered model of the universe.

♦ **1620** The Italian painter Artemisia Gentileschi paints *Judith and Holofernes*.

Glossary

A.D. The letters A.D. stand for the Latin Anno Domini which means "in the year of our Lord." Dates with these letters written after them are measured forward from the year Christ was born.

Almanac A book containing a calendar for the year ahead and other information such as festivals, holidays, and the movements of the planets.

Altarpiece A painting or sculpture placed behind an altar in a church.

Apprentice Someone (usually a young person) legally bound to a craftsman for a number of years in order to learn a craft.

Baptistery Part of a church, or a separate building, where people are baptized.

B.C. Short for "Before Christ." Dates with these letters after them are measured backward from the year of Christ's birth.

Bureaucracy A system of government that relies on a body of officials and usually involves much paperwork and many regulations.

Civil servant A person whose job is to carry out the work of the government.

Classical A term used to describe the civilizations of ancient Greece and Rome, and any later art and architecture based on ancient Greek and Roman examples.

Contemporary Someone or something that lives or exists at the same period of time.

Diet A general assembly of representatives of the Holy Roman Empire who gathered to make decisions and pass laws.

Draper A cloth merchant.

Edict A proclamation or order that has the force of law.

Entrepreneur A business person who is willing to take risks and try something new in order to make money.

Envoy Someone sent abroad to represent the government.

Excommunicate To ban someone from taking part in the rites of the church.

Fresco A type of painting that is usually used for decorating walls and ceilings in which colors are painted into wet plaster.

Guild An association of merchants or craftsmen organized to protect the interests of its members and to regulate the quality of their goods and services.

Heresy A belief that is contrary to the accepted teachings of the church.

Heretic Someone whose beliefs contradict the teachings of the church.

Humanism A new way of thinking about human life that characterized the Renaissance. It was based on study of the "humanities," that is, ancient Greek and Roman texts, history, and philosophy, and stressed the importance of developing rounded, cultured people.

Hundred Years' War A long-drawn-out war between France and England, lasting from 1337 to 1453. It consisted of a series of campaigns with periods of tense peace in between.

Indulgences Cancelations of punishments for sins. Indulgences were often granted by the church in return for money.

Laity or lay people Anyone who is not of the clergy.

Low Countries A region in Europe bordering on the North Sea and comprising present-day Belgium, Luxembourg, and the Netherlands.

Mercenary A soldier who will fight for anyone in return for money.

Patronage The act of ordering and paying for a work of art.

Perspective A technique that allows artists to create the impression of three-dimensional space in their pictures. Near objects are made to appear larger, and far objects are shown smaller.

Propaganda The spreading of ideas or information, which may be true or false, in order to help a particular cause or person.

Psychology The study of the mind. Also, the way a person or group thinks or behaves.

Rate of exchange The amount of money in one currency needed to buy a given amount in another.

Rites The ceremonial acts of the church.

Siege A military blockade of a castle or town to force it to surrender, often by cutting off its food and water.

Speculate To buy or sell goods in the hope of making a profit from price changes.

Strategic Something that is necessary or useful to carry out a plan (often military).

Swiss Confederation An anti-Hapsburg league of Swiss cantons (districts), which formed the basis of present-day Switzerland.

Tempera A type of paint made by mixing powdered pigments (colors) with egg. It was widely used in medieval times and the Renaissance.

Theology The study of religious faith and practice.

Treason The name given to a subject's act of betrayal of their king or queen.

Treatise A book or long essay about the principles, or rules, of a particular subject.

Triptych A picture or carving consisting of three panels side by side. It was often used as an altarpiece.

Triumphal arch A huge, freestanding arch decorated with sculpture built by the ancient Romans to celebrate a great military victory or leader. Processions passed through the arch as part of victory celebrations.

Vatican The headquarters of the pope and papal government in Rome.

Vernacular The language of the ordinary people of a country, rather than a literary or formal language such as Latin.

Further Reading

Ackroyd, Peter. *London: The Biography.* New York: Doubleday, 2001.

Bainton, Roland Herbert. *Here I Stand: A Life of Martin Luther.* New York: Penguin USA, 1995.

Barstow, Anne Llewellyn. *Witchcraze: A New History of the European Witch Hunts.* San Francisco, CA: Harper, 1995.

Batzner, Nike. *Mantegna.* Cologne, Germany: Könemann, 1998.

Bell, Eric Temple. *Men of Mathematics.* New York: Simon & Schuster, 1986.

Bramly, Serge. *Leonardo: The Artist and the Man.* New York: Penguin USA, 1995.

Braudel, Fernand. *The Wheels of Commerce.* Berkeley, CA: University of California Press, 1992.

Brion, Marcel. *The Medici: A Great Florentine Family.* London: Elek, 1969.

Brown, Lloyd Arnold. *The Story of Maps.* New York: Dover Publications, 1979.

Camesasca, Ettore. *Mantegna.* New York: Riverside Books, 1994.

Chamberlin, E. R. *Marguerite of Navarre.* New York: Dial Press, 1974.

Clark, Kenneth. *Leonardo da Vinci.* New York: Penguin USA, 1993.

Cleugh, James. *The Medici.* Garden City, NY: Doubleday, 1975.

Cunnally, John. *Images of the Illustrious.* Princeton, NJ: Princeton University Press, 1999.

Curry, Patrick. *Introducing Machiavelli.* New York: Totem Books, 1996.

Da Vinci, Leonardo. *The Notebooks of Leonardo da Vinci (Volumes 1 and 2).* New York: Dover Publications, 1975.

Ferris, Julie. *Shakespeare's London: A Guide to Elizabethan London.* New York: Larousse Kingfisher Chambers, 2000.

Freedberg, Sydney Joseph. *Painting in Italy, 1500–1600.* New Haven, CT: Yale University Press, 1993.

Gould, Cecil Hilton Monk. *Parmigianino.* New York: Abbeville Press, 1995.

Gullberg, Jan, and Peter Hilton. *Mathematics: From the Birth of Numbers.* New York: W.W. Norton, 1997.

Hauser, Arnold. *Mannerism: The Crisis of the Renaissance and the Origins of Modern Art.* London: Routledge & Paul, 1965.

Joannides, Paul. *Masaccio and Masolino: A Complete Catalogue.* London: Phaidon Press, 1997.

Kallen, Stuart A., and Patti M. Boekhoff. *Leonardo da Vinci.* San Diego, CA: Lucent Books, 2000.

Kapr, Albert. *Johann Gutenberg: The Man and His Invention.* Brookfield, VT: Scholar Press, 1996.

Kent, Dale. *Cosimo de' Medici and the Florentine Renaissance: The Patron's Oeuvre.* New Haven, CT: Yale University Press, 2000.

Knecht, R.J. *Catherine de' Medici.* Reading, MA: Addison-Wesley, 1998.

Levack, Brian P. *The Witch-Hunt in Early Modern Europe.* Reading, MA: Addison-Wesley, 1995.

Mack, Rosamond E. *Bazaar to Piazza: Islamic Trade and Italian Art, 1300–1600.* Berkeley, CA: University of California Press, 2001.

Marani, Pietro C. *Leonardo da Vinci: The Complete Paintings.* New York: Harry N. Abrams, 2000.

Mitchell, Bonner. *Rome in the High Renaissance: The Age of Leo X.* Norman, OK: University of Oklahoma Press, 1973.

Murray, Linda Lefevre. *The High Renaissance and Mannerism: Italy, the North, and Spain, 1500–1600.* London: Thames & Hudson, 1985.

Price, Christine. *Made in the Renaissance, Arts and Crafts of the Age of Exploration.* New York: Dutton, 1963.

Romei, Francesca. *Leonardo da Vinci: Artist, Inventor, and Scientist of the Renaissance.* New York: Peter Bedrick Books, 1994.

Rowdon, Maurice. *Lorenzo the Magnificent.* London: Weidenfeld & Nicolson, 1974.

Runion, Garth E. *Golden Section.* Palo Alto, CA: Dale Seymour Publications, 1990.

Russel, Jeffrey. *A History of Witchcraft: Sorcerers, Heretics, and Pagans.* London: Thames & Hudson, 1982.

Scher, Stephen. *The Currency of Fame: Portrait Medals of the Renaissance.* New York: Harry N. Abrams, 1994.

Siraisi, Nancy G. *Medieval and Early Renaissance Medicine: An Introduction to Knowledge and Practice.* Chicago, IL: University of Chicago Press, 1990.

Smart, Alastair. *The Renaissance and Mannerism in Italy.* London: Thames & Hudson, 1971.

Spike, John T. *Masaccio.* New York: Abbeville Press, 1996.

Stepanek, Sally. *Martin Luther.* Broomall, PA: Chelsea House Publications, 1986.

Strathern, Paul. *Machiavelli in 90 Minutes.* Chicago, IL: Ivan R. Dee, 1998.

Toht, David, and Betony Toht. *Daily Life in Ancient and Modern London.* Minneapolis, MN: Runestone Press, 2001.

Viroli, Maurizio. *Niccolo's Smile: A Biography of Machiavelli.* New York: Farrar Straus & Giroux, 2000.

Walker, D.P. *Spiritual and Demonic Magic.* University Park, PA: Pennsylvania State University Press, 2000.

Whitfield, Peter. *New Found Lands: Maps in the History of Exploration.* London: Routledge, 1998.

Wilford, John Noble. *The Mapmakers.* New York: Knopf, 2000.

Williams, Norman Lloyd. *Tudor London Visited.* London: Cassell, 1991.

WEBSITES

World history site
www.historyworld.net

BBC Online: History
www.bbc.co.uk/history

The Webmuseum's tour of the Renaissance
www.oir.ucf.edu/wm/paint/glo/renaissance/

Virtual time travel tour of the Renaissance
library.thinkquest.org/3588/Renaissance/

The Renaissance
www.learner.org/exhibits/renaissance

National Gallery of Art—tour of 16th-century Italian paintings
www.nga.gov/collection/gallery/ita16.htm

Uffizi Art Gallery, Florence
musa.uffizi.firenze.it/welcomeE.html

Database of Renaissance artists
www.artcyclopedia.com/index.html

Set Index

Numbers in **bold type** are volume numbers.

Page numbers in *italics* refer to pictures or their captions.

Picture Credits

MAPS

The maps in this book show the locations of cities, states, and empires of the
Renaissance period. However, for the sake of clarity, present-day place names are
often used.